# studysync®

## Reading & Writing Companion

## Origin Stories

How does who we were guide who we will become?

studysync.com

Send all inquiries to:
BookheadEd Learning, LLC
610 Daniel Young Drive
Sonoma, CA 95476

ISBN 978-1-94-973903-9

6 7 8 9 LMN 25 24 23 22 21

C

# Student Guide

## Getting Started

Welcome to the StudySync Reading & Writing Companion! In this book, you will find a collection of readings based on the theme of the unit you are studying. As you work through the readings, you will be asked to answer questions and perform a variety of tasks designed to help you closely analyze and understand each text selection. Read on for an explanation of each section of this book.

# Close Reading and Writing Routine

In each unit, you will read texts that share a common theme, despite their different genres, time periods, and authors. Each reading encourages a closer look through questions and a short writing assignment.

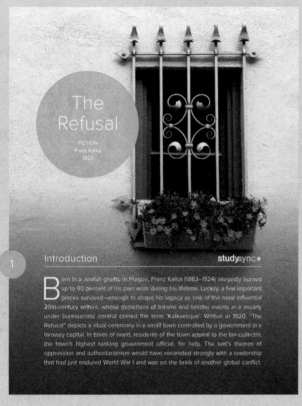

## 1 Introduction

An Introduction to each text provides historical context for your reading as well as information about the author. You will also learn about the genre of the text and the year in which it was written.

## 2 Notes

Many times, while working through the activities after each text, you will be asked to **annotate** or **make annotations** about what you are reading. This means that you should highlight or underline words in the text and use the "Notes" column to make comments or jot down any questions you have. You may also want to note any unfamiliar vocabulary words here.

You will also see sample student annotations to go along with the Skill lesson for that text.

Reading & Writing Companion

# First Read

During your first reading of each selection, you should just try to get a general idea of the content and message of the reading. Don't worry if there are parts you don't understand or words that are unfamiliar to you. You'll have an opportunity later to dive deeper into the text.

# Think Questions

These questions will ask you to start thinking critically about the text, asking specific questions about its purpose, and making connections to your prior knowledge and reading experiences. To answer these questions, you should go back to the text and draw upon specific evidence to support your responses. You will also begin to explore some of the more challenging vocabulary words in the selection.

# Skills

Each Skill includes two parts: Checklist and Your Turn. In the Checklist, you will learn the process for analyzing the text. The model student annotations in the text provide examples of how you might make your own notes following the instructions in the Checklist. In the Your Turn, you will use those same instructions to practice the skill.

**THE REFUSAL**     First Read

Read "The Refusal." After you read, complete the Think Questions below.

## THINK QUESTIONS

1. What can the reader infer about the tax-collector's power? Where does his power come from, and how is it expressed? Use evidence from the text to support your inferences.

2. What do you know about the relationship between the government, located in the faraway capital, and the small town? How do the villagers view the capital and the people who represent it? Cite evidence from the text to support your answer.

3. What role does the ceremony play in life in the small town? How do most townspeople feel about this custom? Support your answer with evidence from the text.

4. Use context clues to determine the meaning of **exceptional** as it is used in paragraph 5. Write your definition here and identify clues that helped you figure out its meaning.

5. Read the following dictionary entry:

   **petition**
   pe·ti·tion /pə'tiSH(ə)n/ *noun*

   1. A formal, written request to an authority
   2. A solemn appeal to a superior
   3. An application to a court for a judicial action

   Which definition most closely matches the meaning of **petition** as it is used in paragraph 5? Write the correct definition of *petition* here and explain how you figured out the meaning.

**CHARACTER**     Skill: Character

Use the Checklist to analyze Character in "The Refusal." Refer to the sample student annotations about Character in the text.

### CHECKLIST FOR CHARACTER

In order to analyze how complex characters develop and interact in a text, note the following:

✓ the traits of complex characters in the text, such as a character that

- has conflicting emotions and motivations
- develops and changes over the course of a story or drama
- advances the events of the plot
- develops the central idea, or theme, through his or her actions

✓ the ways that characters respond, react, or change as the events of the plot unfold and how they interact with other characters in the story

✓ how the reactions and responses of complex characters help to advance the plot and develop the theme

To evaluate how complex characters develop and interact in a text, consider the following questions:

✓ Which characters in the text could be considered complex?

✓ Do the characters change as the plot unfolds? When do they begin to change? Which events cause them to change?

✓ How do any changes the characters undergo help to advance the plot and develop the theme?

### YOUR TURN

1. The narrator's description of the colonel during the reception leads the reader to conclude that—

   ○ A. the colonel is considered to be an ordinary citizen.
   ○ B. the colonel is openly disrespected by the townspeople.
   ○ C. the colonel worries about losing his position as tax-collector.
   ○ D. the colonel inspires great fear among the townspeople.

2. The crowd's reaction to the colonel's refusal reveals that in this society—

   ○ A. the people feel dissatisfied with their government and plan to revolt.
   ○ B. the people are glad that nothing has happened to upset their traditions.
   ○ C. the people recognize that the colonel is a human being just as they are.
   ○ D. the people understand that the colonel is a powerless figurehead.

3. Which detail in the passage most clearly suggests that the colonel's character may be more complex than the townspeople realize?

   ○ A. He silently holds the two symbolic bamboo poles.
   ○ B. He breathes deeply and conspicuously, like a frog.
   ○ C. He drops the bamboo poles and sinks into a chair.
   ○ D. He reveals no emotion during the reception.

# THE REFUSAL — Close Read

Reread "The Refusal." As you reread, complete the Skills Focus questions below. Then use your answers and annotations from the questions to help you complete the Write activity.

## SKILLS FOCUS

1. Paragraph 3 of "The Refusal" contains descriptions of the capital and the small town in which the story is set. Explain what you can infer about how the setting might affect the characters.

2. Analyze the townspeople's attitudes toward the soldiers and the colonel. Use textual evidence to explain what the different attitudes suggest about the characters' roles and interactions in the story.

3. In paragraph 7, the narrator reveals his feelings about the events in the town. Explain what you can infer about his character from this revelation and discuss how the details the narrator supplies help to advance the plot.

4. The young people in the final paragraph of the story are described as "discontent." Explain the likely source of their unhappiness and why this fact helps make them complex.

5. Discuss how the characters in "The Refusal" use language, or avoid using language, and how communication affects the events in the story.

## WRITE

LITERARY ANALYSIS: How does the author use the historical setting to create complex yet believable characters? Choose one or two characters to focus on and use evidence from the text to support your response.

## Roosevelts on the Radio
INFORMATIONAL TEXT

### Introduction

A week after his inauguration, President Franklin Delano Roosevelt gave his first "fireside chat" to the nation over the radio. He, along with First Lady Eleanor, began an unprecedented series of radio addresses delivered directly to the American people. Their influence changed how Americans expect their politicians to communicate.

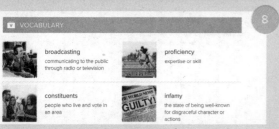

## VOCABULARY

**broadcasting**
communicating to the public through radio or television

**proficiency**
expertise or skill

**constituents**
people who live and vote in an area

**infamy**
the state of being well-known for disgraceful character or actions

---

## 6  Close Read & Skills Focus

After you have completed the First Read, you will be asked to go back and read the text more closely and critically. Before you begin your Close Read, you should read through the Skills Focus to get an idea of the concepts you will want to focus on during your second reading. You should work through the Skills Focus by making annotations, highlighting important concepts, and writing notes or questions in the "Notes" column. Depending on instructions from your teacher, you may need to respond online or use a separate piece of paper to start expanding on your thoughts and ideas.

## 7  Write

Your study of each selection will end with a writing assignment. For this assignment, you should use your notes, annotations, personal ideas, and answers to both the Think and Skills Focus questions. Be sure to read the prompt carefully and address each part of it in your writing.

## 8  English Language Learner

The English Language Learner texts focus on improving language proficiency. You will practice learning strategies and skills in individual and group activities to become better readers, writers, and speakers.

# Extended Writing Project and Grammar

This is your opportunity to use genre characteristics and craft to compose meaningful, longer written works exploring the theme of each unit. You will draw information from your readings, research, and own life experiences to complete the assignment.

## 1 Writing Project

After you have read all of the unit text selections, you will move on to a writing project. Each project will guide you through the process of writing your essay. Student models will provide guidance and help you organize your thoughts. One unit ends with an **Extended Oral Project** which will give you an opportunity to develop your oral language and communication skills.

## 2 Writing Process Steps

There are four steps in the writing process: Plan, Draft, Revise, and Edit and Publish. During each step, you will form and shape your writing project, and each lesson's peer review will give you the chance to receive feedback from your peers and teacher.

## 3 Writing Skills

Each Skill lesson focuses on a specific strategy or technique that you will use during your writing project. Each lesson presents a process for applying the skill to your own work and gives you the opportunity to practice it to improve your writing.

Literary Analysis Writing Process: Plan

PLAN   DRAFT   REVISE   EDIT AND PUBLISH

Skill: Organizing Argumentative Writing

••• CHECKLIST FOR ORGANIZING ARGUMENTATIVE WRITING

As you consider how to organize your writing for your argumentative essay, use the following questions as a guide:

• Have I identified my claim or claims and the evidence that supports it?
• Have I identified reasons for my claim?
• Have I identified any counterclaims that I will need to address?
• Have I identified the textual evidence that will support my reasons?

# Origin Stories

How does who we were guide who we will become?

Genre Focus: **TEXTS THAT BLEND GENRES**

## Texts

 Paired Readings

**1**    Literary Focus: Magical Realism

**6**    The City that Never Stops Giving
POETRY   *Lagnajita Mukhopadhyay*

**9**    Past and Future
POETRY   *Sarojini Naidu*

**11**    The Joy Luck Club
FICTION   *Amy Tan*

**27**    The Best We Could Do: An Illustrated Memoir
INFORMATIONAL TEXT   *Thi Bui*

**44**    Worship the Spirit of Criticism: Address at Pasteur Institute
INFORMATIONAL TEXT   *Louis Pasteur*

**47**    A Very Old Man with Enormous Wings
FICTION   *Gabriel García Márquez (Translated by Gregory Rabassa)*

**60**    The Nose
FICTION   *Nikolai Gogol*

**85**    A Quilt of a Country
INFORMATIONAL TEXT   *Anna Quindlen*

**97**    Creation Myths from Around the World
INFORMATIONAL TEXT   *Angie Shumov*

**101**    Looking for Palestine: Growing Up Confused in an American-Arab Family
INFORMATIONAL TEXT   *Najla Said*

**106**    Coming-of-Age Traditions from Around the World
INFORMATIONAL TEXT   *Ursula Villarreal-Moura*

# Extended Writing Project and Grammar

**118**    Plan

*Planning Research*
*Evaluating Sources*
*Research and Notetaking*

**135**    Draft

*Critiquing Research*
*Paraphrasing*
*Sources and Citations*
*Print and Graphic Features*

**148**    Revise

*Using a Style Guide*
*Grammar: Conjunctive Adverbs*
*Grammar: Commonly Misspelled Words*

**157**    Edit and Publish

## English Language Learner Resources

**159**    Tiger Moms and Trophies for Everyone: How Culture Influences Parenting
**INFORMATIONAL TEXT**

**169**    Karima
**DRAMA**

**187**    Text Fulfillment through StudySync

# Unit 6: Origin Stories

## How does who we were guide who we will become?

### NIKOLAI GOGOL

Nikolai Gogol (1809–1852) was born in Ukraine to a gentleman farmer who also wrote Ukrainian folk comedies. Gogol would become a central figure of 19th-century Russian literature, known for his use of absurd humor and surrealism in the bizarre social and political satires that shaped his novels, plays, and short stories. One of his best-known short stories, "The Nose" (1836), presents an unflattering portrayal of Russian aristocratic society.

### GABRIEL GARCÍA MÁRQUEZ

Although he's known for his contributions to the literary genre known as magical realism, Gabriel García Márquez (1927–2014) has said that there's not a single line in all of his work that does not have a basis in reality. One of the main life events that would shape his writing style was revisiting the place where he was born, a small town near the Caribbean coast in Colombia, when he was twenty-two. He said of his visit, "It was as if everything I saw had already been written."

### SAROJINI NAIDU

Poet and political activist Sarojini Naidu (1879–1949) was the first Indian woman to become president of the Indian National Congress, the political party founded in 1885 that led the movement for independence from Great Britain. With Mahatma Gandhi, Naidu opposed British colonial rule in India, serving multiple prison sentences for her anti-British activity. Also a writer and intellectual, Naidu published her first volume of poetry, *The Golden Threshold*, in 1905.

### LOUIS PASTEUR

The contributions of French chemist and microbiologist Louis Pasteur (1822–1895) to the fields of science, technology, and medicine in the 19th century were fundamental to the emergence of modern science. Out of the research he conducted on microorganisms and infectious diseases, he developed various vaccines and a process for eliminating pathogens from food, known as pasteurization. In his 1888 address to his colleagues, Pasteur emphasized the importance of constantly questioning one's scientific findings.

### ANNA QUINDLEN

As a native New Yorker and a journalist, who at one point had been a staff writer for *The New York Times*, Anna Quindlen (b. 1952) was greatly affected by the 9/11 terrorist attacks when they happened. Published just weeks after the attacks, her piece "A Quilt of a Country" (2001) reflects on the state of the nation at that time, and calls for the preservation of American values such as unity, equality, and tolerance.

### NAJLA SAID

Although writer and actress Najla Said (b. 1974) was born in Boston to a Palestinian father and a Lebanese mother, she was baptized Episcopalian. As the daughter of famed intellectual Edward Said, she grew up around world-renowned scholars and frequent political debates. Yet attending a private girls' school in New York's wealthy Upper East Side, she often just wanted to fit in with her peers. Said's memoir follows her journey of self-discovery, framing it within the context of America's fraught relationship with the Middle East.

### AMY TAN

Born in Oakland, California, to Chinese immigrant parents, Amy Tan (b. 1952) was inspired to write her first novel, *The Joy Luck Club* (1989), when she visited China for the first time with her mother. An often humorous portrayal of family dynamics across generations and cultures, the novel incorporates semi-autobiographical material, family stories, and traditions. Tan's many books often draw from her own family history in their depictions of Chinese American women and the immigrant experience.

### URSULA VILLARREAL-MOURA

Born and raised in San Antonio, Texas, Ursula Villarreal-Moura (b. 1978) writes fiction and essays dealing with personal and family history, relationships, and identity, and has said that her writing often addresses themes of loss and abandonment. In her essay, "Coming-of-Age Traditions from Around the World," Villarreal-Moura surveys a wide range of coming-of-age rituals from China to Mexico and the United States to the Amazon.

### THI BUI

Thi Bui (b. 1975) was born three months before the end of the Vietnam War and fled with her family to the United States in 1978 after the fall of South Vietnam. Bui has said that her illustrated memoir, *The Best We Could Do* (2017), was a way for her to make sense of the stories she heard growing up. The book contextualizes her parents' anecdotes within a broader political and historical narrative, and recalls the difficulties she and her family faced as immigrants in the United States.

### LAGNAJITA MUKHOPADHYAY

At seventeen, Lagnajita Mukhopadhyay (b. 1998) became Nashville, Tennessee's first Youth Poet Laureate. An immigrant from India, she is committed to increasing the visibility of the diverse backgrounds and experiences that make up American culture. While Mukhopadhyay has played various instruments and has written songs from a young age, she thinks of her poetry as having a different function in that it can be a means of broadening the worldview of her readers.

### ANGIE SHUMOV

Angie Shumov's article "Creation Myths from Around the World" delves into the narratives told across cultures and throughout history about the origins of the world. It discusses the myths of ancient civilizations, in addition to the commonalities among the origin stories of Christianity, Judaism, and Islam.

# Introduction

This informational text provides readers with cultural and historical background information about the origins of magical realist literature. Magical realism, at first only a term used to describe art, became its own literary genre in the 1940s. Used to describe literature that blends the real with the supernatural, magical realism often shares characteristics with other genres such as surrealism. Literary giants Isabel Allende and Gabriel García Márquez are some of the most well-known authors of magical realism, with their masterpieces *The House of the Spirits* and *One Hundred Years of Solitude*. Discover how writers of magical realism play with time and metaphor, to lend attention to political and social structures in the real world.

# "Time is elastic and ever changing in works of magical realism."

1 Have you ever had a dream that felt completely real? Perhaps you dreamed you were in a familiar place, like home or school. Then suddenly you realized that you were flying or breathing underwater and your sense of time seemed to stretch and bend. If these things happened in real life, they'd be mind-blowing, but in a dream, they seem perfectly natural. Magical realism is a form of literature that resembles a dreamlike state. Magical realism is a genre of narrative fiction and film that blends the real and the magical in a totally believable way.

**The Origins of Magical Realism**

2 Before magical realism became an official literary movement, authors experimented with bending reality. In his 1915 novella *The Metamorphosis*, the Czech novelist Franz Kafka describes how the main character, Gregor Samsa, deals with the fact that he has turned into an insect overnight. Readers accustomed to realistic fiction might wonder, "Did the man really turn into a bug?" It doesn't matter, because the narrator and the main character believe that he has. In treating the story's conflict in this matter-of-fact way, Kafka blurred the lines between the real and the unreal in a way that hadn't been done before outside of mythology or tales of fantasy.

3 The term *magical realism* was introduced ten years later by the German art critic Franz Roh, who used it to describe art that injected bizarre images into **realistic** depictions of the world. Literary magical realism originated in Latin America beginning in the 1940s. It is a genre primarily associated with the works of a group of writers from that region. They include Cuban Alejo Carpentier, Colombian Gabriel García Márquez, Argentines Julio Cortázar and Jorge Luis Borges, and Chilean Isabel Allende. Cortázar's *Rayuela* (Hopscotch) (1963) and García Márquez's *One Hundred Years of Solitude* (1970) are considered two of the first major novels of magical realism. Translations of these and other works spread the influence of magical realism around the world. Toni Morrison, Alice Hoffman, and Salman Rushdie have incorporated magical realism into their novels, as have filmmakers like Guillermo del Toro. His films *The Devil's Backbone* and *Pan's Labyrinth* tell dark stories that blend myth and fantasy with the reality of their wartime

Please note that excerpts and passages in the StudySync® library and this workbook are intended as touchstones to generate interest in an author's work. The excerpts and passages do not substitute for the reading of entire texts, and StudySync® strongly recommends that students seek out and purchase the whole literary or informational work in order to experience it as the author intended. Links to online resellers are available in our digital library. In addition, complete works may be ordered through an authorized reseller by filling out and returning to StudySync® the order form enclosed in this workbook.

Reading & Writing Companion    1

NOTES

settings. Magical realism also inspired artists, such as Italian painter Giorgio de Chirico and American painter Philip Evergood, both of whom blended realist and surrealist aspects to evoke a dreamlike reality.

Giorgio de Chirico, Italian painter, among some of his works, 1925.

**Timely and Timeless Stories**

4   Magical realists were influenced by folk and fairy tales, mythology, and the literary movements of early twentieth century European writers, especially the writings of Kafka. Their works—mostly stories and novels—are characterized by complicated plots that weave together the **mundane**, the magical, and the political. Time is elastic and ever-changing in works of magical realism. It might jump forward or backward or even stand still for long stretches. The settings are often ordinary places where **supernatural** events happen to characters who have magical qualities. For example, in García Márquez's story "The Handsomest Drowned Man in the World," the women in a fishing village fall in love with and adopt a sailor whose dead body has washed ashore. A character in Isabel Allende's multigenerational novel *The House of the Spirits* has green hair and yellow eyes. The **fantastical** events in magical realist literature are often metaphorical. They disguise an implicit critique of social or political institutions. For example, neither the villagers nor the priests in García Márquez's story "A Very Old Man With Enormous Wings" treat the angel with much respect. The angel himself is the antithesis of angelic; he's smelly, grumpy, and uncommunicative. García Márquez seems to be commenting on the traditional ideas about religion.

5   Another feature of magical realism is its **indifferent** tone. Narrators describe real and fantastical events with a lack of surprise. They are not impressed or amazed by the fantastical elements in the story. As a result, the readers follow their lead, taking the surreal events in stride and treating them as perfectly ordinary and normal.

NOTES

*Dowager in a Wheelchair* (1952) by Philip Evergood.

## Overlaps with Other Genres

6   Magical realism, which is also sometimes known as magic realism, shares
    many qualities with other literary genres from the modern and postmodern
    periods, including surrealism and, fantasy. Like surrealism, magical realism
    borrows archetypes and inexplicable and fantastical elements from the world
    of dreams; however, in magical realism, their purpose is to comment on the
    external world, not to explore the author's inner psyche. Like fantasy, magical
    realism borrows supernatural events and fantastical characters from myth,
    folklore, and fairy tales, but magical realism lacks fantasy's sense of wonder
    and impossibility, replacing it with a tone of indifference.

7 **Major Concepts**

- Magical realism incorporates elements of mythology, folktales, fairy tales, and fantasy.

- The stories, novels, and films in the magical realist tradition have plots that blend the surreal and fantastical and the real and mundane. Neither the characters, the narrator, nor the readers question the supernatural elements that arise in the stories.

- The mundane settings and supernatural elements in the stories often provide cover for a critique of social, cultural, or political institutions.

8 **Style**

- Literary works of magical realism primarily take the form of novels and stories.

- These works feature realistic and mundane settings that serve as the backdrop for magical or even surreal events and characters with fantastical traits.

- The works have a realistic tone. The narrators tell the story in a straightforward, almost indifferent manner. Magical events are described as if they are ordinary and normal.

- Time is often not linear in works of magical realism. It may bend, skip forward or backward, or stand still.

9 Magical realism is a thoughtful blend of the everyday and the surreal, the serious and the supernatural. Since the 1960s, readers have been enthralled by magical realists' stories of love and death set in mundane yet magical villages. The original authors of magical realistic literature have mostly passed away, yet they have left a powerful legacy behind. Where do you see elements of magical realism in the books, stories, films, and videos you read and watch?

# Literary Focus

Read "Literary Focus: Magical Realism." After you read, complete the Think Questions below.

## ☁ THINK QUESTIONS

1. What are several early influences on the literary movement of magical realism? Be sure to cite evidence directly from the text.

2. How do the elements of magical realism help disguise its critique of social or political institutions?

3. Based on your reading of the text, what effect does the blending of the mundane and the magical have on the readers of magical realism?

4. Use context clues to determine the meaning of the word **indifferent**. Write your best definition, along with the words and phrases that were most helpful in determining the word's meaning. Then, check a dictionary to confirm your understanding.

5. The word *supernatural* comes from the Latin *super*, meaning "above" or "beyond" and *naturalis*, meaning "birth." With this information in mind, write your best definition of the word **supernatural** as it used in this text. Cite any words or phrases that were particularly helpful in coming to your conclusion.

Please note that excerpts and passages in the StudySync® library and this workbook are intended as touchstones to generate interest in an author's work. The excerpts and passages do not substitute for the reading of entire texts, and StudySync® strongly recommends that students seek out and purchase the whole literary or informational work in order to experience it as the author intended. Links to online resellers are available in our digital library. In addition, complete works may be ordered through an authorized reseller by filling out and returning to StudySync® the order form enclosed in this workbook.

Reading & Writing Companion

5

# The City that Never Stops Giving

POETRY
Lagnajita Mukhopadhyay
2015

## Introduction

Poet and avid guitar-player Lagnajita Mukhopadhyay was born in India, and as a child moved with her family to Nashville, Tennessee. In 2015, at the age of 17, she published a book of poetry, *This is Our War*, and was named Nashville's first Youth Poet Laureate. Her poem "The City that Never Stops Giving" was inspired by the location of her high school in downtown Nashville, and captures the buzz and energy of a major urban area, at once particular and universal.

# "From this crosswalk, electricity ripples through the crooked streets of the city."

1   The city never stops giving
2   on the corner of 6th and Broadway
3   where downtown traffic is a **harrowing**
4   consistency, when the light turns green,
5   it doesn't always mean go.
6   Where Roy Orbison wrote "Oh Pretty Woman[1],"
7   emboldened by the femme[2] of mercy
8   below his apartment balcony
9   where tourists and the music
10  leave a warm taste of **affinity**,
11  by the Starbucks in the Renaissance[3]
12  that snags money from teenagers
13  who **rendezvous** before school.
14  They never spell my name right
15  on the little cups filled with magic.
16  From this crosswalk, electricity ripples
17  through the crooked streets of the city.
18  The paths of headlights **mature** into veins
19  of a breathing atmosphere.
20  The wait is forgiving, and when
21  we don't like what we see and
22  all significance is lost, we turn
23  around softly and walk the other way.
24  A newfangled[4] story in a blink and a sigh,
25  blinkers signaling a right turn,
26  people staring straight ahead,
27  headlong into the bright eyes
28  of a **symmetrical** world. So begins
29  the journey across the black and white,
30  when everyone becomes familiar

---

1. **"Oh Pretty Woman"** a hit 1964 song performed by Roy Orbison
2. **femme** woman
3. **Renaissance** the name of a building
4. **newfangled** fancy or modern, objectionably so

NOTES

31 and nothing feels strange. Every step
32 falls into the heartbeats of a million
33 lonely people, and when the crosswalk ends,
34 so does another chance encounter
35 with a supreme stranger that you
36 never would have otherwise met—
37 a James, a Taylor, a small life changer,
38 the old love of a never ending family
39 meets the new love of a never ending home,
40 and the city never stops giving.

"The City that Never Stops Giving" by Ladnajita Mukhopadhyay, 2015 Nashville Youth Poet Laureate. Used by permission of the National Youth Poet Laureate Program, www.youthlaureate.org.

## ✏ WRITE

PERSONAL RESPONSE: In her poem "The City that Never Stops Giving," poet Lagnajita Mukhopadhyay's speaker offers a personal guide to Nashville, Tennessee. In response to this poem, write a poem or short prose piece of your own, entitled, "The [Place] that _____," in which you guide readers in how to see the bond you have with the place where you live or have grown up. Include descriptive details, figurative language, and other elements to create a rich and meaningful response.

# Past and Future

POETRY
Sarojini Naidu
1905

## Introduction

Known as "the Nightingale of India," Sarojini Naidu (1879–1949) was an activist, poet, and politician. She was a strong proponent of the Indian Congress Movement, led by Mahatma Gandhi, which opposed British rule and called for Indian independence in the years surrounding the Second World War. She became the first Indian female president of the National Congress in 1925. The subjects of her poems, many of which she composed and published prior to her activism, range from patriotism to ancient wisdom. In "Past and Future," published in Naidu's first collection of poems, *The Golden Threshold*, she personifies the "Soul," depicting its transition from old memories to new beginnings.

# "The new hath come and now the old retires. . ."

NOTES

1   The new hath come and now the old retires:
2   And so the past becomes a mountain-cell,
3   Where lone, apart, old hermit-memories dwell
4   In **consecrated** calm, forgotten yet
5   Of the keen heart that hastens to forget
6   Old longings in fulfilling new desires.

7   And now the Soul stands in a **vague**, intense
8   Expectancy and **anguish** of suspense,
9   On the dim chamber-threshold . . . lo! he sees
10  Like a strange, fated bride as yet unknown,
11  His **timid** future shrinking there alone,
12  Beneath her marriage-veil of mysteries.

Sarojini Naidu and Mahatma Gandhi on their way to break the Salt Laws in India, 1930.

## ✏ WRITE

LITERARY ANALYSIS: For some, the past is something to be escaped, while for others, it is something to long for. Which is it for the speaker of this poem? Locate poetic elements and identify structural techniques in the text to support your interpretation.

# The Joy Luck Club

FICTION
Amy Tan
1989

## Introduction

Chinese American author Amy Tan (b. 1952) grew up in Oakland, California, as the daughter of immigrant parents. *The Joy Luck Club*, her first published book, was a critical and commercial success that catapulted her into the literary mainstream. Constructed of episodic stories drawing on her own heritage, the book explores the relationships between a group of Chinese American women and their immigrant mothers, offering a compelling portrait of their interwoven lives across generations. In the story presented here, "Two Kinds," a mother has high expectations for her daughter, hoping she will become "a Chinese Shirley Temple" or a classically trained pianist on *The Ed Sullivan Show*.

# "For unlike my mother, I did not believe I could be anything I wanted to be. I could only be me."

NOTES

Skill: Textual
Evidence

*The mother wants her daughter to succeed when she says, "you can be prodigy" and "best anything." She is competing with Auntie Lindo to have the best daughter when she says, "Her daughter, she is only best tricky."*

"Jing-Mei Woo: Two Kinds"

1    My mother believed you could be anything you wanted to be in America. You could open a restaurant. You could work for the government and get good retirement. You could buy a house with almost no money down. You could become rich. You could become instantly famous.

2    "Of course you can be prodigy[1], too," my mother told me when I was nine. "You can be best anything. What does Auntie Lindo know? Her daughter, she is only best tricky."

3    America was where all my mother's hopes lay. She had come here in 1949 after losing everything in China: her mother and father, her family home, her first husband, and two daughters, twin baby girls. But she never looked back with regret. There were so many ways for things to get better.

              . . .

4    We didn't immediately pick the right kind of prodigy. At first my mother thought I could be a Chinese Shirley Temple[2]. We'd watch Shirley's old movies on TV as though they were training films. My mother would poke my arm and say, "*Ni kan*"—You watch. And I would see Shirley tapping her feet, or singing a sailor song, or pursing her lips into a very round O while saying, "Oh my goodness."

5    "*Ni kan*," said my mother as Shirley's eyes flooded with tears. "You already know how. Don't need talent for crying!"

6    Soon after my mother got this idea about Shirley Temple, she took me to the beauty training school in the Mission district and put me in the hands of a student who could barely hold the scissors without shaking. Instead of getting

---

1. **prodigy** an exceptionally talented child or young person
2. **Shirley Temple** a child star in the 1930s, Shirley Temple (1928–2014) became a diplomat and was ambassador to Czechoslovakia during the fall of the Berlin Wall

big fat curls, I **emerged** with an uneven mass of crinkly black fuzz. My mother dragged me off to the bathroom and tried to wet down my hair.

7    "You look like Negro Chinese," she lamented, as if I had done this on purpose.

8    The instructor of the beauty training school had to lop off these soggy clumps to make my hair even again. "Peter Pan is very popular these days" the instructor assured my mother. I now had hair the length of a boy's, with straight-across bangs that hung at a slant two inches above my eyebrows. I liked the haircut and it made me actually look forward to my future fame.

9    In fact, in the beginning, I was just as excited as my mother, maybe even more so. I pictured this prodigy part of me as many different images, trying each one on for size. I was a dainty ballerina girl standing by the curtains, waiting to hear the right music that would send me floating on my tiptoes. I was like the Christ child lifted out of the straw manger, crying with holy indignity. I was Cinderella stepping from her pumpkin carriage with sparkly cartoon music filling the air.

10    In all of my imaginings, I was filled with a sense that I would soon become *perfect*. My mother and father would adore me. I would be beyond reproach. I would never feel the need to sulk for anything.

11    But sometimes the prodigy in me became impatient. "If you don't hurry up and get me out of here, I'm disappearing for good," it warned. "And then you'll always be nothing."

12    Every night after dinner my mother and I would sit at the Formica kitchen table. She would present new tests, taking her examples from stories of amazing children she had read in *Ripley's Believe It or Not*, or *Good Housekeeping*, *Reader's Digest*, and a dozen other magazines she kept in a pile in our bathroom. My mother got these magazines from people whose houses she cleaned. And since she cleaned many houses each week, we had a great assortment. She would look through them all, searching for stories about remarkable children.

13    The first night she brought out a story about a three-year-old boy who knew the capitals of all the states and even most of the European countries. A teacher was quoted as saying that the little boy could also pronounce the names of the foreign cities correctly.

14    "What's the capital of Finland?" my mother asked me, looking at the magazine story.

15   All I knew was the capital of California, because Sacramento was the name of the street we lived on in Chinatown. "Nairobi!" I guessed, saying the most foreign word I could think of. She checked to see if that was possibly one way to pronounce "Helsinki" before showing me the answer.

16   The tests got harder—multiplying numbers in my head, finding the queen of hearts in a deck of cards, trying to stand on my head without using my hands, predicting the daily temperatures in Los Angeles, New York, and London.

17   One night I had to look at a page from the Bible for three minutes and then report everything I could remember. "Now Jehoshaphat had riches and honor in abundance and... that's all I remember, Ma," I said.

18   And after seeing my mother's disappointed face once again, something inside me began to die. I hated the tests, the raised hopes and failed expectations. Before going to bed that night, I looked in the mirror above the bathroom sink and when I saw only my face staring back—and that it would always be this ordinary face—I began to cry. Such a sad, ugly girl! I made high-pitched noises like a crazed animal, trying to scratch out the face in the mirror.

19   And then I saw what seemed to be the prodigy side of me—a face I had never seen before. I looked at my reflection, blinking so I could see more clearly. The girl staring back at me was angry, powerful. This girl and I were the same. I had new thoughts, willful thoughts, or rather thoughts filled with lots of won'ts. I won't let her change me, I promised myself. I won't be what I'm not.

20   So now on nights when my mother presented her tests, I performed listlessly, my head propped on one arm. I pretended to be bored. And I was. I got so bored I started counting the bellows of the foghorns out on the bay while my mother drilled me in other areas. The sound was comforting and reminded me of the cow jumping over the moon. And the next day, I played a game with myself, seeing if my mother would give up on me before eight bellows. After a while I usually counted only one, maybe two bellows at most. At last she was beginning to give up hope.

21   Two or three months went by without any mention of my being a prodigy. And then one day my mother was watching *The Ed Sullivan Show* on TV. The TV was old and the sound kept shorting out. Every time my mother got halfway up from the sofa to adjust the set, the sound would go back on and Ed would be talking. As soon as she sat down, Ed would go silent again. She got up, the TV broke into loud piano music. She sat down. Silence. Up and down, back and forth, quiet and loud. It was like a stiff embraceless dance between her and the TV set. Finally she stood by the set with her hand on the sound dial.

22  She seemed entranced by the music, a little frenzied piano piece with this mesmerizing quality, sort of quick passages and then teasing lilting ones before it returned to the quick playful parts.

23  "*Ni kan*," my mother said, calling me over with hurried hand gestures. "Look here."

24  I could see why my mother was fascinated by the music. It was being pounded out by a little Chinese girl, about nine years old, with a Peter Pan haircut. The girl had the sauciness of a Shirley Temple. She was proudly modest like a proper Chinese child. And she also did this fancy sweep of a curtsy, so that the fluffy skirt of her white dress cascaded slowly to the floor like the petals of a large carnation.

25  In spite of these warning signs, I wasn't worried. Our family had no piano and we couldn't afford to buy one, let alone reams of sheet music and piano lessons. So I could be generous in my comments when my mother bad-mouthed the little girl on TV.

26  "Play note right, but doesn't sound good! No singing sound," complained my mother.

27  "What are you picking on her for?" I said carelessly. "She's pretty good. Maybe she's not the best, but she's trying hard." I knew almost immediately that I would be sorry I had said that.

28  "Just like you," she said. "Not the best. Because you not trying." She gave a little huff as she let go of the sound dial and sat down on the sofa.

29  The little Chinese girl sat down also, to play an encore of "Anitra's Tanz," by Grieg. I remember the song, because later on I had to learn how to play it.

30  Three days after watching *The Ed Sullivan Show* my mother told me what my schedule would be for piano lessons and piano practice. She had talked to Mr. Chong, who lived on the first floor of our apartment building. Mr. Chong was a retired piano teacher and my mother had traded housecleaning services for weekly lessons and a piano for me to practice on every day, two hours a day, from four until six.

31  When my mother told me this, I felt as though I had been sent to hell. I whined and then kicked my foot a little when I couldn't stand it anymore.

32  "Why don't you like me the way I am? I'm *not* a genius! I can't play the piano. And even if I could, I wouldn't go on TV if you paid me a million dollars!" I cried.

33 My mother slapped me. "Who ask you to be genius?" she shouted. "Only ask you be your best. For you sake. You think I want you to be genius? Hnnh! What for! Who ask you!"

34 "So ungrateful," I heard her mutter in Chinese, "If she had as much talent as she has temper, she'd be famous now."

35 Mr. Chong, whom I secretly nicknamed Old Chong, was very strange, always tapping his fingers to the silent music of an invisible orchestra. He looked ancient in my eyes. He had lost most of the hair on the top of his head and he wore thick glasses and had eyes that always looked tired and sleepy. But he must have been younger that I thought, since he lived with his mother and was not yet married.

36 I met Old Lady Chong once and that was enough. She had this peculiar smell like a baby that had done something in its pants. And her fingers felt like a dead person's, like an old peach I once found in the back of the refrigerator; the skin just slid off the meat when I picked it up.

37 I soon found out why Old Chong had retired from teaching piano. He was deaf. "Like Beethoven!" he shouted to me. "We're both listening only in our head!" And he would start to **conduct** his frantic silent sonatas.

38 Our lessons went like this. He would open the book and point to different things, explaining their purpose: "Key! Treble! Bass! No sharps or flats! So this is C major! Listen now and play after me!"

39 And then he would play the C scale a few times, a simple chord, and then, as if inspired by an old, unreachable itch, he gradually added more notes and running trills and a pounding bass until the music was really something quite grand.

40 I would play after him, the simple scale, the simple chord, and then I just played some nonsense that sounded like a cat running up and down on top of garbage cans. Old Chong smiled and applauded and then said, "Very good! But now you must learn to keep time!"

41 So that's how I discovered that Old Chong's eyes were too slow to keep up with the wrong notes I was playing. He went through the motions in half-time. To help me keep rhythm, he stood behind me, pushing down on my right shoulder for every beat. He balanced pennies on top of my wrists so that I would keep them still as I slowly played scales and arpeggios. He had me curve my hand around an apple and keep that shape when playing chords. He marched stiffly to show me how to make each finger dance up and down, staccato like an obedient little soldier.

42 He taught me all these things, and that was how I also learned I could be lazy and get away with mistakes, lots of mistakes. If I hit the wrong notes because I hadn't practiced enough, I never corrected myself. I just kept playing in rhythm. And Old Chong kept conducting his own private reverie.

43 So maybe I never really gave myself a fair chance. I did pick up the basics pretty quickly, and I might have become a good pianist at the young age. But I was so determined not to try, not to be anybody different that I learned to play only the most ear-splitting preludes, the most discordant hymns.

44 Over the next year, I practiced like this, dutifully in my own way. And then one day I heard my mother and her friend Lindo Jong both talking in a loud bragging tone of voice so others could hear. It was after church, and I was leaning against the brick wall wearing a dress with stiff white petticoats. Auntie Lindo's daughter, Waverly, who was about my age, was standing farther down the wall about five feet away. We had grown up together and shared all the closeness of two sisters **squabbling** over crayons and dolls. In other words, for the most part, we hated each other. I thought she was snotty. Waverly Jong had gained a certain amount of fame as "Chinatown's Littlest Chinese Chess Champion."

45 "She bring home too many trophy," lamented Auntie Lindo that Sunday. "All day she play chess. All day I have no time do nothing but dust off her winnings." She threw a scolding look at Waverly, who pretended not to see her.

46 "You lucky you don't have this problem," Auntie Lindo said with a sigh to my mother.

47 And my mother squared her shoulders and bragged: "Our problem worser than yours. If we ask Jing-mei wash dish, she hear nothing but music. It's like you can't stop this natural talent."

48 And right then, I was determined to put a stop to her foolish pride.

49 A few weeks later, Old Chong and my mother conspired to have me play in a talent show which would be held in the church hall. By then, my parents had saved up enough to buy me a secondhand piano, a black Wurlitzer spinet with a scarred bench. It was the showpiece of our living room.

50 For the talent show, I was to play a piece called "Pleading Child," from Schumann's *Scenes from Childhood*. It was a simple, moody piece that sounded more difficult than it was. I was supposed to memorize the whole thing, playing the repeat parts twice to make the piece sound longer. But I dawdled over it, playing a few bars and then cheating, looking up to see what

Please note that excerpts and passages in the StudySync® library and this workbook are intended as touchstones to generate interest in an author's work. The excerpts and passages do not substitute for the reading of entire texts, and StudySync® strongly recommends that students seek out and purchase the whole literary or informational work in order to experience it as the author intended. Links to online resellers are available in our digital library. In addition, complete works may be ordered through an authorized reseller by filling out and returning to StudySync® the order form enclosed in this workbook.

Reading & Writing Companion    17

NOTES

notes followed. I never really listened to what I was playing. I daydreamed about being somewhere else, about being someone else.

51     The part I liked to practice best was the fancy curtsy: right foot out, touch the rose on the carpet with a pointed foot, sweep to the side, left leg bends, look up and smile.

52     My parents invited all the couples from the Joy Luck Club[3] to witness my debut. Auntie Lindo and Uncle Tin were there. Waverly and her two older brothers had also come. The first two rows were filled with children both younger and older than I was. The littlest ones got to go first. They recited simple nursery rhymes, squawked out tunes on miniature violins, twirled Hula Hoops, practiced in pink ballet tutus, and when they bowed or curtsied, the audience would sigh in unison, "Awww," and then clap enthusiastically.

53     When my turn came, I was very confident. I remember my childish excitement. It was as if I knew, without a doubt, that the prodigy side of me really did exist. I had no fear whatsoever, no nervousness. I remember thinking to myself, This is it! This is it! I looked out over the audience, at my mother's blank face, my father's yawn, Auntie Lindo's stiff-lipped smile, Waverly's sulky expression. I had on a white dress layered with sheets of lace, and a pink bow in my Peter Pan haircut. As I sat down I envisioned people jumping to their feet and Ed Sullivan rushing up to introduce me to everyone on TV.

54     And I started to play. It was so beautiful. I was so caught up in how lovely I looked that at first I didn't worry about how I would sound. So it was a surprise to me when I hit the first wrong note and I realized something didn't sound quite right. And then I hit another and another followed that. A chill started at the top of my head and began to trickle down. Yet I couldn't stop playing, as though my hands were bewitched. I kept thinking my fingers would adjust themselves back, like a train switching to the right track. I played this strange jumble through two repeats, the sour notes staying with me all the way to the end.

55     When I stood up, I discovered my legs were shaking. Maybe I had just been nervous and the audience, like Old Chong, had seen me go through the right motions and had not heard anything wrong at all. I swept my right foot out, went down on my knee, looked up and smiled. The room was quiet, except for Old Chong, who was beaming and shouting "Bravo! Bravo! Well done!" But then I saw my mother's face, her stricken face. The audience clapped weakly, and as I walked back to my chair, with my whole face quivering as I

---

3. **the Joy Luck Club** the name of the mahjong club organized by the four immigrant Chinese women whose stories comprise *The Joy Luck Club*, Amy Tan's debut novel

tried not to cry, I heard a little boy whisper loudly to his mother, "That was awful," and mother whispered back, "Well, she certainly tried."

56 And now I realized how many people were in the audience, the whole world it seemed. I was aware of eyes burning into my back. I felt the shame of my mother and father as they sat stiffly through the rest of the show.

57 We could have escaped during intermission. Pride and some strange sense of honor must have anchored my parents to their chairs. And so we watched it all: the eighteen-year-old boy with a fake mustache who did a magic show and juggled flaming hoops while riding a unicycle. The breasted girl with white makeup who sang from *Madama Butterfly* and got honorable mention. And the eleven-year-old boy who won first prize playing a tricky violin song that sounded like a busy bee.

58 After the show, the Hsus, the Jongs, and the St. Clairs from the Joy Luck Club came up to my mother and father.

59 "Lots of talented kids," Auntie Lindo said vaguely, smiling broadly.

60 "That was somethin' else," my father said, and I wondered if he was referring to me in a humorous way, or whether he even remembered what I had done.

61 Waverly looked at me and shrugged her shoulders. "You aren't a genius like me," she said matter-of-factly. And if I hadn't felt so bad, I would have pulled her braids and punched her stomach.

62 But my mother's expression was what devastated me: a quiet, blank look that said she had lost everything. I felt the same way, and it seemed as if everybody were now coming up, like gawkers at the scene of an accident, to see what parts were actually missing. When we got on the bus to go home, my father was humming the busy-bee tune and my mother was silent. I kept thinking she wanted to wait until we got home before shouting at me. But when my father unlocked the door to our apartment, my mother walked in and then went to the back, into the bedroom. No accusations. No blame. And in a way, I felt disappointed. I had been waiting for her to start shouting, so that I could shout back and cry and blame her for all my misery.

63 I assumed my talent-show fiasco meant I never had to play the piano again. But two days later, after school, my mother came out of the kitchen and saw me watching TV.

64 "Four clock," she reminded me as if it were any other day. I was stunned, as though she were asking me to go through the talent-show torture again. I wedged myself more tightly in front of the TV.

65   "Turn off TV," she called from the kitchen five minutes later.

66   I didn't budge. And then I decided. I didn't have to do what mother said anymore. I wasn't her slave. This wasn't China. I had listened to her before and look what happened. She was the stupid one.

67   She came out of the kitchen and stood in the arched entryway of the living room. "Four clock," she said once again, louder.

68   "I'm not going to play anymore," I said nonchalantly. "Why should I? I'm not a genius."

69   She walked over and stood in front of the TV. I saw that her chest was heaving up and down in an angry way.

70   "No!" I said, and I now felt stronger, as if my true self had finally emerged. So this was what had been inside me all along.

71   "No! I won't!" I screamed.

72   She yanked me by the arm, pulled me off the floor, snapped off the TV. She was frighteningly strong, half pulling, half carrying me towards the piano as I kicked the throw rugs under my feet. She lifted me up onto the hard bench. I was sobbing by now, looking at her bitterly. Her chest was heaving even more and her mouth was open, smiling crazily as if she were pleased that I was crying.

73   "You want me to be someone that I'm not!" I sobbed. "I'll never be the kind of daughter you want me to be!"

74   "Only two kinds of daughters," she shouted in Chinese. "Those who are obedient and those who follow their own mind! Only one kind of daughter can live in this house. Obedient daughter!"

75   "Then I wish I wasn't your daughter. I wish you weren't my mother," I shouted. As I said these things I got scared. It felt like worms and toads and slimy things crawling out of my chest, but it also felt good, as if this awful side of me had surfaced, at last.

76   "Too late to change this," said my mother shrilly.

77   And I could sense her anger rising to its breaking point. I wanted to see it spill over. And that's when I remembered the babies she had lost in China, the ones we never talked about. "Then I wish I'd never been born!" I shouted. "I wish I were dead! Like them."

78   It was as if I had said magic words. Alakazam!—and her face went blank, her mouth closed, her arms went **slack**, and she backed out of the room, stunned, as if she were blowing away like a small brown leaf, thin, brittle, lifeless.

. . .

79   It was not the only disappointment my mother felt in me. In the years that followed, I failed her so many times, each time asserting my own will, my right to fall short of expectations. I didn't get straight As. I didn't become class president. I didn't get into Stanford. I dropped out of college.

80   For unlike my mother, I did not believe I could be anything I wanted to be. I could only be me.

81   And for all those years, we never talked about the disaster at the recital or my terrible accusations afterward at the piano bench. All that remained unchecked, like a betrayal that was now unspeakable. So I never found a way to ask her why she had hoped for something so large that failure was **inevitable**.

82   And even worse, I never asked her what frightened me the most: Why had she given up hope?

83   For after our struggle at the piano, she never mentioned my playing again. The lessons stopped. The lid to the piano was closed, shutting out the dust, my misery, and her dreams.

84   So she surprised me. A few years ago, she offered to give me the piano, for my thirtieth birthday. I had not played in all those years. I saw the offer as a sign of forgiveness, a tremendous burden removed.

85   "Are you sure?" I asked shyly. "I mean, won't you and Dad miss it?"

86   "No, this your piano," she said firmly. "Always your piano. You only one can play."

87   "Well, I probably can't play anymore," I said. "It's been years."

88   "You pick up fast," said my mother, as if she knew this was certain. "You have natural talent. You could been genius if you want to."

89   "No, I couldn't."

90   "You just not trying," said my mother. And she was neither angry nor sad. She said it as if to announce a fact that could never be disproved. "Take it," she said.

91 But I didn't at first. It was enough that she had offered it to me. And after that, every time I saw it in my parents' living room, standing in front of the bay windows, it made me feel proud, as if it were a shiny trophy that I had won back.

92 Last week I sent a tuner over to my parents' apartment and had the piano reconditioned, for purely sentimental reasons. My mother had died a few months before and I had been been getting things in order for my father, a little bit at a time. I put the jewelry in special silk pouches. The sweaters she had knitted in yellow, pink, bright orange—all the colors I hated—I put those in moth-proof boxes. I found some old Chinese silk dresses, the kind with little slits up the sides. I rubbed the old silk against my skin, then wrapped them in tissue and decided to take them home with me.

93 After I had the piano tuned, I opened the lid and touched the keys. It sounded even richer than I remembered. Really, it was a very good piano. Inside the bench were the same exercise notes with handwritten scales, the same secondhand music books with their covers held together with yellow tape.

94 I opened up the Schumann book to the dark little piece I had played at the recital. It was on the left-hand side of the page, "Pleading Child." It looked more difficult than I remembered. I played a few bars, surprised at how easily the notes came back to me.

95 And for the first time, or so it seemed, I noticed the piece on the right-hand side. It was called "Perfectly Contented." I tried to play this one as well. It had a lighter melody but the same flowing rhythm and turned out to be quite easy. "Pleading Child" was shorter but slower; "Perfectly Contented" was longer but faster. And after I played them both a few times, I realized they were two halves of the same song.

---

"Two Kinds" from THE JOY LUCK CLUB by Amy Tan, copyright © 1989 by Amy Tan. Used by permission of G. P. Putnam's Sons, an imprint of Penguin Publishing Group, a division of Penguin Random House LLC. All rights reserved.

# First Read

Read *The Joy Luck Club*. After you read, complete the Think Questions below.

## ☁ THINK QUESTIONS

1. What does the mother in the excerpt want from her daughter? Use details from the text to support your answer.

2. How does the narrator's attitude toward the idea of being a prodigy change over the course of the text? Support your answer with evidence from the text.

3. After her performance at the piano recital, explain why the narrator is disappointed when her mother does not yell at her. Support your answer using ideas from the text that are directly stated or implied.

4. Use context clues to determine the meaning of the word **squabble** as it is used in the text. Write your definition of *squabble*, and explain which clues helped you understand it.

5. Keeping in mind that the Latin word *evitar* means "to avoid," and the Latin prefix *in-* means "not," write your definition of the word **inevitable** as it is used in the text. Then, use a print or an online dictionary to verify your understanding.

# Skill:
# Textual Evidence

Use the Checklist to analyze Textual Evidence in *The Joy Luck Club*. Refer to the sample student annotation about Textual Evidence in the text.

## ••• CHECKLIST FOR TEXTUAL EVIDENCE

In order to support an analysis by citing evidence that is explicitly stated in the text, do the following:

✓ Read the text closely and critically.

✓ Identify what the text says explicitly.

✓ Find the most relevant textual evidence that supports your analysis.

✓ Consider why an author explicitly states specific details and information.

✓ Cite the specific words, phrases, sentences, or paragraphs from the text that support your analysis.

In order to interpret implicit meanings in a text by making inferences, do the following:

✓ Combine information directly stated in the text with your own knowledge, experiences, and observations.

✓ Cite the specific words, phrases, sentences, or paragraphs from the text that led to and support this inference.

In order to cite textual evidence to support an analysis of what the text says explicitly as well as inferences drawn from the text, consider the following questions:

✓ Have I read the text closely and critically?

✓ What inferences am I making about the text?

✓ What textual evidence am I using to support these inferences?

✓ Am I quoting the evidence from the text correctly?

✓ Does my textual evidence logically relate to my analysis or the inference I am making?

# Skill:
# Textual Evidence

Reread paragraphs 12–20 of *The Joy Luck Club*. Then, using the Checklist on the previous page, answer the multiple-choice questions below.

## ⟳ YOUR TURN

1. The textual evidence that best supports the inference that Jing-mei is not a prodigy is —

   ○ A. "My mother got these magazines from people whose houses she cleaned. And since she cleaned many houses each week, we had a great assortment. She would look through them all, searching for stories about remarkable children."

   ○ B. "All I knew was the capital of California, because Sacramento was the name of the street we lived on in Chinatown. "Nairobi!" I guessed, saying the most foreign word I could think of."

   ○ C. "The tests got harder—multiplying numbers in my head, finding the queen of hearts in a deck of cards, trying to stand on my head without using my hands, predicting the daily temperatures in Los Angeles, New York, and London."

   ○ D. "And after seeing my mother's disappointed face once again, something inside me began to die."

2. Which of the interpretations below is best supported by textual evidence in paragraphs 19 and 20?

   ○ A. Jing-mei realizes that she has no idea who she truly is.

   ○ B. Jing-mei is frightened by how angry her mother has made her with the endless tests.

   ○ C. Jing-mei realizes that the power to resist her mother makes her a kind of prodigy.

   ○ D. Jing-mei promises herself that she will continue to try her best with her mother's tests.

# Close Read

Reread *The Joy Luck Club*. As you reread, complete the Skills Focus questions below. Then use your answers and annotations from the questions to help you complete the Write activity.

## ◎ SKILLS FOCUS

1. Irony occurs when the author reveals an outcome that is not what readers or characters are expecting (situational irony), or uses language to mean the opposite of what is literally stated in order to create humor (verbal irony). Identify an example of irony in the text and cite evidence to explain what makes the example ironic.

2. Identify a scene in which the daughter's upbringing conflicts with her mother's. Explain why she chooses to reject her mother's influence and the effect this has on the theme.

3. Explain the central plot as well as how the author weaves in other reflections or events to help develop and enrich the narrative. Discuss the effect(s) the structure creates.

4. Reread the last two paragraphs of the story. Analyze the conclusion to discuss the theme that a person's past informs his or her identity in the present.

## ✎ WRITE

LITERARY ANALYSIS: This excerpt from the novel is titled "Two Kinds: Jing-Mei Woo." How does the idea of being "two kinds" posed in the title of this excerpt provide insight into the narrator's character? In your response, cite textual evidence to trace the development of this complex character over the course of the text.

# The Best We Could Do:
## An Illustrated Memoir

INFORMATIONAL TEXT
Thi Bui
2017

## Introduction

After Thi Bui moved across the continental United States to be closer to her aging parents, she came to understand the cold distance between them. In her bestselling illustrated memoir, *The Best We Could Do*, Bui recounts her family's nautical escape from Vietnam in 1978 and her roots in that war-scarred country, "thinking that," she writes, "if I bridged the gap between the past and the present I could fill the void between my parents and me." In this excerpt from her National Book Critics Circle finalist book, Bui articulates the ways "proximity and closeness are not the same."

# "I keep looking toward the past, tracing our journey in reverse . . ."

**Page 1**

I notice big waves and a swaying boat that suggest a dangerous journey from Vietnam to the United States. The first voiceover explains the context, while the second shares the adult Bui's self-deprecating point of view.

**Page 2**

 Skill:
Media

The harsh sound of the moving truck and the worried look on Bui's face show her anxiety about moving to be closer to her parents. The fourth panel emphasizes the emotional distance between them.

**Page 4**

Please note that excerpts and passages in the StudySync® library and this workbook are intended as touchstones to generate interest in an author's work. The excerpts and passages do not substitute for the reading of entire texts, and StudySync® strongly recommends that students seek out and purchase the whole literary or informational work in order to experience it as the author intended. Links to online resellers are available in our digital library. In addition, complete works may be ordered through an authorized reseller by filling out and returning to StudySync® the order form enclosed in this workbook.

Reading & Writing Companion

31

**Page 5**

**Page 7**

Please note that excerpts and passages in the StudySync® library and this workbook are intended as touchstones to generate interest in an author's work. The excerpts and passages do not substitute for the reading of entire texts, and StudySync® strongly recommends that students seek out and purchase the whole literary or informational work in order to experience it as the author intended. Links to online resellers are available in our digital library. In addition, complete works may be ordered through an authorized reseller by filling out and returning to StudySync® the order form enclosed in this workbook.

Reading & Writing Companion    35

**Page 9**

Reading & Writing Companion

**Page 11**

**Page 12**

The Best We Could Do by Thi Bui. Copyright (c) 2017 Thi Bui. Used with the permission of Express Permissions on behalf of Abrams ComicArts, an imprint of Harry N. Abrams, Inc., New York. All rights reserved. www.abramsbooks.com

# First Read

Read *The Best We Could Do*. After you read, complete the Think Questions below.

 **THINK QUESTIONS**

1. Why does Bui feel guilty? What does this guilt reveal about her and the situation she is in? Cite evidence from the text to support your response.

2. How is Bui's relationship with her mother different from Bui's relationship with her father? What do both relationships have in common? Explain, citing examples from the text in support of your response.

3. Explain what you learned about the relationship between Bui's father and his father, citing evidence from the text.

4. Use context clues to determine the meaning of the word **chasm** as it is used in the excerpt. Write your definition and identify clues that helped you figure out its meaning.

5. Use context clues to determine the meaning of the word **origin** as it is used in the excerpt. Write your definition of *origin*, along with those words and phrases from the text that helped you determine its meaning.

# Skill:
# Media

Use the Checklist to analyze Media in *The Best We Could Do*. Refer to the sample student annotations about Media in the text.

In order to determine the representation of a subject or a key scene in two different artistic mediums, do the following:

✓ Note the artistic medium and its features.

✓ Identify what is emphasized or absent in each treatment of a subject or a key scene.

✓ Examine why the same subject receives completely different treatments in different media.

✓ Consider sources, as a story about a historical event might refer, directly or indirectly, to letters, paintings, plays, or photographs from the same place and time as the events that took place.

To analyze the representation of a subject or a key scene in two different artistic mediums, including what is emphasized or absent in each treatment, consider the following questions:

✓ Is the content informational or fictional? How does this affect the treatment of the key scene or subject?

✓ What are the strengths and weaknesses of each artistic medium? How does this affect the treatment of the key scene or subject?

✓ What is emphasized and what is absent, or left out of each medium's version of events?

Please note that excerpts and passages in the StudySync® library and this workbook are intended as touchstones to generate interest in an author's work. The excerpts and passages do not substitute for the reading of entire texts, and StudySync® strongly recommends that students seek out and purchase the whole literary or informational work in order to experience it as the author intended. Links to online resellers are available in our digital library. In addition, complete works may be ordered through an authorized reseller by filling out and returning to StudySync® the order form enclosed in this workbook.

Reading & Writing Companion     41

# Skill:
# Media

Reread pages 7–8 of *The Best We Could Do*. Then, using the Checklist on the previous page, answer the multiple-choice questions below.

## ⟳ YOUR TURN

1. This question has two parts. First, answer Part A. Then, answer Part B.

   **Part A:** The voiceover on the bottom panel on page 7 indicates that—

   ○ A. the narrator feels incomplete because of her lack of knowledge about her heritage.
   ○ B. the narrator made a decision to get a large tattoo of Vietnam on her back.
   ○ C. Vietnam is now more important to the author than her parents are.
   ○ D. the narrator finally cares about Vietnam the way her parents do.

   **Part B:** Which of the following images best connects to the voiceovers to support your answer from Part A?

   ○ A. the waves behind her
   ○ B. the Vietnam-shaped hole in her back
   ○ C. the image of her writing
   ○ D. her hair blowing in the wind

2. The illustration of the narrator and her mother in the first panel on page 8 and the voiceovers in all of the panels on page 8 work together to illustrate the idea that—

   ○ A. the narrator's mother remembers the boat trip from Vietnam to America.
   ○ B. she finds an ocean-front view helps her remember Vietnam.
   ○ C. the ocean is behind everything the narrator thinks about.
   ○ D. there is distance between Bui and her mother.

# Close Read

Reread *The Best We Could Do*. As you reread, complete the Skills Focus questions below. Then use your answers and annotations from the questions to help you complete the Write activity.

## ◎ SKILLS FOCUS

1. Analyze how the illustrations and the text work together to develop the memoir, including what is emphasized in each depiction of events.

2. Identify the central or main idea of the memoir and analyze its development over the course of the text.

3. On the second page of the graphic memoir, the narrator notes that "proximity and closeness are not the same." Discuss the denotations of each word, the connotations of the words, and analyze how the nuances of the word meanings affect your understanding of the text.

4. Analyze the memoir to explain how the text and illustrations show the impact of the past on the present life of the author.

## ✎ WRITE

INFORMATIVE: In this graphic novel excerpt, author Thi Bui illustrates the sacrifices her family made in their search for a better future. Create your own illustrated memoir, in your writer's notebook or in a digital format, about a time in your life where you or your family made a sacrifice. Be sure that elements of your illustrated memoir work together to convey a distinct tone and central idea. Then, write a response explaining how you used elements of media to communicate meaning. Support your response with evidence from the text you created.

Please note that excerpts and passages in the StudySync® library and this workbook are intended as touchstones to generate interest in an author's work. The excerpts and passages do not substitute for the reading of entire texts, and StudySync® strongly recommends that students seek out and purchase the whole literary or informational work in order to experience it as the author intended. Links to online resellers are available in our digital library. In addition, complete works may be ordered through an authorized reseller by filling out and returning to StudySync® the order form enclosed in this workbook.

Reading & Writing Companion   **43**

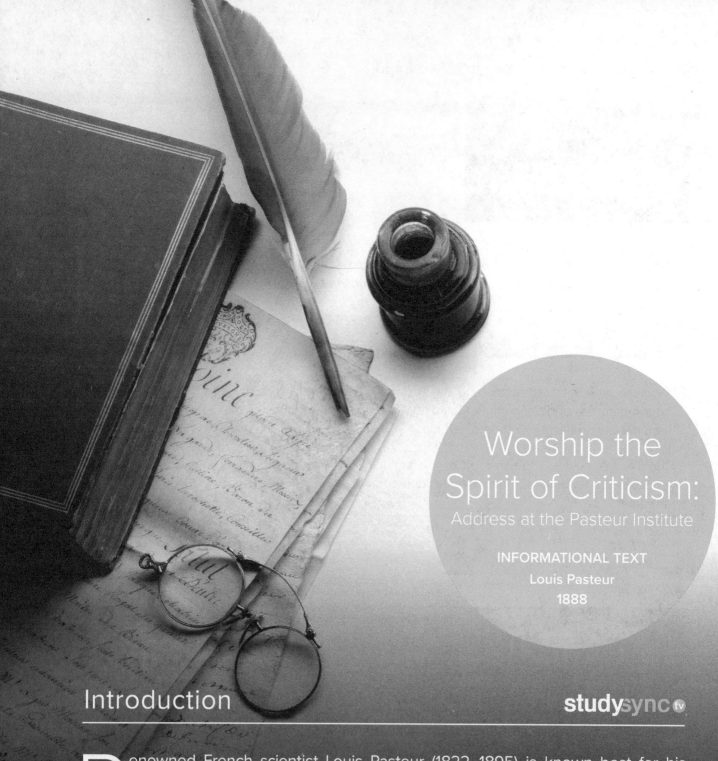

# Worship the Spirit of Criticism:
## Address at the Pasteur Institute

INFORMATIONAL TEXT
Louis Pasteur
1888

## Introduction

Renowned French scientist Louis Pasteur (1822–1895) is known best for his trailblazing research into infectious diseases, which has led to longer and healthier lives for millions of people. On November 14, 1888, he addressed his colleagues at the opening of the Pasteur Institute in Paris. In an effort to encourage the advancement of science, Pasteur exhorted his peers to "worship the spirit of criticism" by questioning their own findings. Pasteur's speech also helped define the relationship between science and society as he pressed future generations of scientists to seek "new means of delivering man from the scourges which beset him."

# "Never advance anything that cannot be proved in a simple and decisive fashion."

*Excerpt from a speech by Louis Pasteur given in 1888 on the occasion of the opening of the Pasteur Institute[1] in Paris:*

Portrait of Louis Pasteur

1   It is now finished, this great building, of which it might be said that there is not a stone but what is the material sign of a generous thought. All the virtues have subscribed to build this dwelling place for work.

2   Alas! mine is the bitter grief that I enter it, a man "vanquished by time," deprived of my masters, even of my companions in the struggle, Dumas, Bouley, Paul Bert, and lastly Vulpian, who, after having been with you, my dear Grancher[2], my counselor at the very first, became the most energetic, the most convinced champion of this method[3].

3   However, if I have the sorrow of thinking that they are no more, after having valiantly taken their part in discussions which I have never provoked but I have had to endure; if they cannot hear me proclaim all that I owe to their counsels and support; if I feel their absence as deeply as on the morrow of their death, I have at least the consolation of believing that all we struggled for together will not perish. The collaborators and students who are now here share our scientific faith.... Keep your early enthusiasm, dear **collaborators**, but let it ever be regulated by rigorous examinations and tests. Never advance anything that cannot be proved in a simple and decisive fashion.

---

1. **Pasteur Institute**  a French research foundation established in 1888 to study biology and microorganisms
2. **Grancher**  Jacques-Joseph Grancher (1843–1907) was a French microbiologist who made significant advances in the treatment of tuberculosis and rabies
3. **this method**  referring to the scientific method, a process for experimentation and testing hypotheses with evidence

NOTES

4    Worship the spirit of criticism. If reduced to itself, it is not an awakener of ideas or a **stimulant** to great things, but, without it, everything is **fallible**; it always has the last word. What I am now asking you, and you will ask of your pupils later on, is what is most difficult to an inventor.

5    It is indeed a hard task, when you believe you have found an important scientific fact and are feverishly anxious to publish it, to constrain yourself for days, weeks, years sometimes, to fight with yourself, to try and ruin your own experiments and only to proclaim your discovery after having exhausted all contrary hypotheses.

6    But when, after so many efforts, you have at last arrived at a certainty, your joy is one of the greatest which can be felt by a human soul, and the thought that you have contributed to the honor of your country renders that joy still deeper.

7    If science has no country, the scientist should have one, and ascribe to it the influence which his works may have in this world.... Two contrary laws seem to be wrestling with each other nowadays; the one, a law of blood and death, ever imagining new means of destruction and forcing nations to be constantly ready for the battlefield—the other, a law of peace, work and health, ever evolving new means of delivering man from the **scourges** which beset him.

8    The one seeks violent conquests; the other, the relief of humanity. The latter places one human life above any victory; while the former would sacrifice hundreds and thousands of lives to the **ambition** of one. The law of which we are the instruments seeks, even in the midst of carnage, to cure the sanguinary ills of the law of war; the treatment inspired by our sanguinary methods may preserve thousands of soldiers. Which of those two laws will **ultimately** prevail, God alone knows. But we may assert that French science will have tried, by obeying the law of humanity, to extend the frontiers of life.

✏ WRITE

RHETORICAL ANALYSIS: How does Louis Pasteur use rhetorical devices to persuade his audience of his purpose and point of view? In your response, be sure to identify Pasteur's audience and purpose, and analyze several examples of rhetorical devices he uses to achieve his purpose.

# A Very Old Man with Enormous Wings

FICTION
Gabriel García Márquez
(Translated by Gregory Rabassa)
1955

## Introduction

Colombian author Gabriel García Márquez (1927–2014) is renowned as a literary giant of the 20th century. He is praised as one of the fathers of magical realism, a style in which the natural and supernatural are woven together with vivid detail. His novels and short stories often reveal deep truths hidden in universal human experiences, such as solitude—a recurring theme in many of his works. In one of his most anthologized short stories, "A Very Old Man with Enormous Wings," García Márquez provides subtle social commentary as he narrates the story of a peculiar man who captivates a small village.

# "The world had been sad since Tuesday."

Skill: Point of View

*García Márquez, the author, is Colombian. Details such as the crabs, the name "Pelayo," and the courtyard suggest a culture from outside the US. The comment about the world shows an omniscient narrator.*

1   On the third day of rain they had killed so many crabs inside the house that Pelayo had to cross his drenched courtyard and throw them into the sea, because the newborn child had a temperature all night and they thought it was due to the stench. The world had been sad since Tuesday. Sea and sky were a single ash-gray thing and the sands of the beach, which on March nights glimmered like powdered light, had become a stew of mud and rotten shellfish. The light was so weak at noon that when Pelayo was coming back to the house after throwing away the crabs, it was hard for him to see what it was that was moving and groaning in the rear of the courtyard. He had to go very close to see that it was an old man, a very old man, lying face down in the mud, who, in spite of his tremendous efforts, couldn't get up, impeded by his enormous wings.

2   Frightened by that nightmare, Pelayo ran to get Elisenda, his wife, who was putting compresses on the sick child, and he took her to the rear of the courtyard. They both looked at the fallen body with a mute stupor. He was dressed like a ragpicker. There were only a few faded hairs left on his bald skull and very few teeth in his mouth, and his pitiful condition of a drenched great-grandfather took away any sense of grandeur he might have had. His huge buzzard wings, dirty and half-plucked, were forever entangled in the mud. They looked at him so long and so closely that Pelayo and Elisenda very soon overcame their surprise and in the end found him familiar. Then they dared speak to him, and he answered in an incomprehensible dialect with a strong sailor's voice. That was how they skipped over the inconvenience of the wings and quite intelligently concluded that he was a lonely castaway from some foreign ship wrecked by the storm. And yet, they called in a neighbor woman who knew everything about life and death to see him, and all she needed was one look to show them their mistake.

3   "He's an angel," she told them. "He must have been coming for the child, but the poor fellow is so old that the rain knocked him down."

4   On the following day everyone knew that a flesh-and-blood angel was held captive in Pelayo's house. Against the judgment of the wise neighbor woman, for whom angels in those times were the fugitive survivors of a celestial

conspiracy, they did not have the heart to club him to death. Pelayo watched over him all afternoon from the kitchen, armed with his bailiff's club, and before going to bed he dragged him out of the mud and locked him up with the hens in the wire chicken coop. In the middle of the night, when the rain stopped, Pelayo and Elisenda were still killing crabs. A short time afterward the child woke up without a fever and with a desire to eat. Then they felt **magnanimous** and decided to put the angel on a raft with fresh water and provisions for three days and leave him to his fate on the high seas. But when they went out into the courtyard with the first light of dawn, they found the whole neighborhood in front of the chicken coop having fun with the angel, without the slightest reverence, tossing him things to eat through the openings in the wire as if he weren't a supernatural creature but a circus animal.

5    Father Gonzaga arrived before seven o'clock, alarmed at the strange news. By that time onlookers less frivolous than those at dawn had already arrived and they were making all kinds of conjectures concerning the captive's future. The simplest among them thought that he should be named mayor of the world. Others of sterner mind felt that he should be promoted to the rank of five-star general in order to win all wars. Some visionaries hoped that he could be put to stud in order to implant the earth a race of winged wise men who could take charge of the universe. But Father Gonzaga, before becoming a priest, had been a robust woodcutter. Standing by the wire, he reviewed his catechism in an instant and asked them to open the door so that he could take a close look at that pitiful man who looked more like a huge decrepit hen among the fascinated chickens. He was lying in the corner drying his open wings in the sunlight among the fruit peels and breakfast leftovers that the early risers had thrown him. Alien to the **impertinences** of the world, he only lifted his antiquarian[1] eyes and murmured something in his dialect when Father Gonzaga went into the chicken coop and said good morning to him in Latin. The parish priest had his first suspicion of an imposter when he saw that he did not understand the language of God or know how to greet His ministers. Then he noticed that seen close up he was much too human: he had an unbearable smell of the outdoors, the back side of his wings was strewn with parasites and his main feathers had been mistreated by terrestrial winds, and nothing about him measured up to the proud dignity of angels. Then he came out of the chicken coop and in a brief sermon warned the curious against the risks of being ingenuous. He reminded them that the devil had the bad habit of making use of carnival tricks in order to confuse the unwary. He argued that if wings were not the essential element in determining the difference between a hawk and an airplane, they were even less so in the recognition of angels. Nevertheless, he promised to write a letter to his bishop so that the latter would write his primate so that the latter would write to the Supreme Pontiff in order to get the final verdict from the highest courts.

Skill: Point of View

*The appearance of a priest and an angel, along with the desire to put the angel into positions of power, show the culture is religious. The narrator judges, perhaps humorously, "less frivolous," "simplest," and "sterner."*

---

1.  **antiquarian**  relating to antiques or a person who collects or specializes in them

6   His **prudence** fell on sterile hearts. The news of the captive angel spread with such rapidity that after a few hours the courtyard had the bustle of a marketplace and they had to call in troops with fixed bayonets to disperse the mob that was about to knock the house down. Elisenda, her spine all twisted from sweeping up so much marketplace trash, then got the idea of fencing in the yard and charging five cents admission to see the angel.

7   The curious came from far away. A traveling carnival arrived with a flying acrobat who buzzed over the crowd several times, but no one paid any attention to him because his wings were not those of an angel but, rather, those of a sidereal bat. The most unfortunate invalids on earth came in search of health: a poor woman who since childhood has been counting her heartbeats and had run out of numbers; a Portuguese man who couldn't sleep because the noise of the stars disturbed him; a sleepwalker who got up at night to undo the things he had done while awake; and many others with less serious ailments. In the midst of that shipwreck disorder that made the earth tremble, Pelayo and Elisenda were happy with fatigue, for in less than a week they had crammed their rooms with money and the line of pilgrims waiting their turn to enter still reached beyond the horizon.

8   The angel was the only one who took no part in his own act. He spent his time trying to get comfortable in his borrowed nest, befuddled by the hellish heat of the oil lamps and sacramental candles that had been placed along the wire. At first they tried to make him eat some mothballs, which, according to the wisdom of the wise neighbor woman, were the food prescribed for angels. But he turned them down, just as he turned down the papal lunches that the penitents brought him, and they never found out whether it was because he was an angel or because he was an old man that in the end ate nothing but eggplant mush. His only supernatural virtue seemed to be patience. Especially during the first days, when the hens pecked at him, searching for the stellar parasites that proliferated in his wings, and the cripples pulled out feathers to touch their defective parts with, and even the most merciful threw stones at him, trying to get him to rise so they could see him standing. The only time they succeeded in arousing him was when they burned his side with an iron for branding steers, for he had been motionless for so many hours that they thought he was dead. He awoke with a start, ranting in his hermetic[2] language and with tears in his eyes, and he flapped his wings a couple of times, which brought on a whirlwind of chicken dung and lunar dust and a gale of panic that did not seem to be of this world. Although many thought that his reaction had not been one of rage but of pain, from then on they were careful not to annoy him, because the majority understood that his passivity was not that of a hero taking his ease but that of a cataclysm in **repose**.

---

2. **hermetic** ascribing to an old, non-scientific belief system composed of elements of astrology, alchemy, and speculation of the afterlife

Copyright © BookheadEd Learning, LLC

9    Father Gonzaga held back the crowd's frivolity with formulas of maidservant inspiration while awaiting the arrival of a final judgment on the nature of the captive. But the mail from Rome showed no sense of urgency. They spent their time finding out if the prisoner had a navel, if his dialect had any connection with Aramaic, how many times he could fit on the head of a pin, or whether he wasn't just a Norwegian with wings. Those meager letters might have come and gone until the end of time if a providential event had not put and end to the priest's tribulations.

10    It so happened that during those days, among so many other carnival attractions, there arrived in the town the traveling show of the woman who had been changed into a spider for having disobeyed her parents. The admission to see her was not only less than the admission to see the angel, but people were permitted to ask her all manner of questions about her absurd state and to examine her up and down so that no one would ever doubt the truth of her horror. She was a frightful tarantula the size of a ram and with the head of a sad maiden. What was most heartrending, however, was not her outlandish shape but the sincere affliction with which she recounted the details of her misfortune. While still practically a child she had sneaked out of her parents' house to go to a dance, and while she was coming back through the woods after having danced all night without permission, a fearful thunderclap rent the sky in two and through the crack came the lightning bolt of brimstone that changed her into a spider. Her only nourishment came from the meatballs that charitable souls chose to toss into her mouth. A spectacle like that, full of so much human truth and with such a fearful lesson, was bound to defeat without even trying that of a haughty angel who scarcely deigned to look at mortals. Besides, the few miracles attributed to the angel showed a certain mental disorder, like the blind man who didn't recover his sight but grew three new teeth, or the paralytic who didn't get to walk but almost won the lottery, and the leper whose sores sprouted sunflowers. Those consolation miracles, which were more like mocking fun, had already ruined the angel's reputation when the woman who had been changed into a spider finally crushed him completely. That was how Father Gonzaga was cured forever of his insomnia and Pelayo's courtyard went back to being as empty as during the time it had rained for three days and crabs walked through the bedrooms.

11    The owners of the house had no reason to lament. With the money they saved they built a two-story mansion with balconies and gardens and high netting so that crabs wouldn't get in during the winter, and with iron bars on the windows so that angels wouldn't get in. Pelayo also set up a rabbit warren close to town and gave up his job as a bailiff for good, and Elisenda bought

Skill:
Summarizing

Summary: A spider-woman arrives with a traveling show. She recounts how this happened to her. The townspeople are moved because the woman explains herself; they feel the angel is behaving as if he is above them.

Please note that excerpts and passages in the StudySync® library and this workbook are intended as touchstones to generate interest in an author's work. The excerpts and passages do not substitute for the reading of entire texts, and StudySync® strongly recommends that students seek out and purchase the whole literary or informational work in order to experience it as the author intended. Links to online resellers are available in our digital library. In addition, complete works may be ordered through an authorized reseller by filling out and returning to StudySync® the order form enclosed in this workbook.

Reading & Writing
Companion

51

some satin pumps with high heels and many dresses of iridescent silk, the kind worn on Sunday by the most desirable women in those times. The chicken coop was the only thing that didn't receive any attention. If they washed it down with creolin and burned tears of myrrh inside it every so often, it was not in homage to the angel but to drive away the dungheap stench that still hung everywhere like a ghost and was turning the new house into an old one. At first, when the child learned to walk, they were careful that he not get too close to the chicken coop. But then they began to lose their fears and got used to the smell, and before the child got his second teeth he'd gone inside the chicken coop to play, where the wires were falling apart. The angel was no less standoffish with him than with the other mortals, but he tolerated the most ingenious infamies with the patience of a dog who had no illusions. They both came down with the chicken pox at the same time. The doctor who took care of the child couldn't resist the temptation to listen to the angel's heart, and he found so much whistling in the heart and so many sounds in his kidneys that it seemed impossible for him to be alive. What surprised him most, however, was the logic of his wings. They seemed so natural on that completely human organism that he couldn't understand why other men didn't have them too.

12 When the child began school it had been some time since the sun and rain had caused the collapse of the chicken coop. The angel went dragging himself about here and there like a stray dying man. They would drive him out of the bedroom with a broom and a moment later find him in the kitchen. He seemed to be in so many places at the same time that they grew to think that he'd be duplicated, that he was reproducing himself all through the house, and the exasperated and unhinged Elisenda shouted that it was awful living in that hell full of angels. He could scarcely eat and his antiquarian eyes had also become so foggy that he went about bumping into posts. All he had left were the bare cannulae of his last feathers. Pelayo threw a blanket over him and extended him the charity of letting him sleep in the shed, and only then did they notice that he had a temperature at night, and was **delirious** with the tongue twisters of an old Norwegian. That was one of the few times they became alarmed, for they thought he was going to die and not even the wise neighbor woman had been able to tell them what to do with dead angels.

13 And yet he not only survived his worst winter, but seemed improved with the first sunny days. He remained motionless for several days in the farthest corner of the courtyard, where no one would see him, and at the beginning of December some large, stiff feathers began to grow on his wings, the feathers of a scarecrow, which looked more like another misfortune of

decrepitude. But he must have known the reason for those changes, for he was quite careful that no one should notice them, that no one should hear the sea chanteys that he sometimes sang under the stars. One morning Elisenda was cutting some bunches of onions for lunch when a wind that seemed to come from the high seas blew into the kitchen. Then she went to the window and caught the angel in his first attempts at flight. They were so clumsy that his fingernails opened a furrow in the vegetable patch and he was on the point of knocking the shed down with the ungainly flapping that slipped on the light and couldn't get a grip on the air. But he did manage to gain altitude. Elisenda let out a sigh of relief, for herself and for him, when she watched him pass over the last houses, holding himself up in some way with the risky flapping of a senile vulture. She kept watching him even when she was through cutting the onions and she kept on watching until it was no longer possible for her to see him, because then he was no longer an annoyance in her life but an imaginary dot on the horizon of the sea.

Gabriel Garcia Marquez. "Un señor muy viejo con unas alas enormes", La increíble y triste historia de la cándida Erendira y de se abuela desalmada. © Gabriela García Márquez, 1972 and Heirs of Gabriel García Márquez. All pages from "A VERY OLD MAN WITH ENORMOUS WINGS" from LEAF STORM AND OTHER STORIES by GABRIEL GARCIA MARQUEZ. Translated by Gregory Rabassa. Copyright © 1971 by Gabriel García Márquez. Reprinted by permission of HarperCollins Publishers.

Please note that excerpts and passages in the StudySync® library and this workbook are intended as touchstones to generate interest in an author's work. The excerpts and passages do not substitute for the reading of entire texts, and StudySync® strongly recommends that students seek out and purchase the whole literary or informational work in order to experience it as the author intended. Links to online resellers are available in our digital library. In addition, complete works may be ordered through an authorized reseller by filling out and returning to StudySync® the order form enclosed in this workbook.

Reading & Writing
Companion

53

# First Read

Read "A Very Old Man with Enormous Wings." After you read, complete the Think Questions below.

## ☁ THINK QUESTIONS

1. What are the townspeople's first impressions of the old man? How do they interpret his appearance? Cite specific evidence from the text to support your answer.

2. What happens when the people learn of the "spider-woman"? How does their reaction compare to when they first discovered the old man? Make sure to include examples from the story.

3. How does the old man transform physically throughout the story? Use specific examples from the text to support your answer.

4. Use the surrounding context to infer the definition of **impertinences** as it is used in paragraph 5 of the story. Write your definition, explaining how you came to this meaning. Then, verify your understanding of the word with a print or an online dictionary.

5. The Latin word *prudentia* is translated "foresight, or practical judgment." Keeping this in mind, come up with your best definition of the word **prudence** as it is used in paragraph 6. Write your definition, and explain which clues led you to arrive at it.

# Skill:
# Point of View

Use the Checklist to analyze Point of View in "A Very Old Man with Enormous Wings." Refer to the sample student annotations about Point of View in the text.

## ••• CHECKLIST FOR POINT OF VIEW

In order to identify the point of view or cultural experience reflected in a work of literature from outside the United States, note the following:

✓ the country of origin of the characters or speaker and author

✓ scenes and details that reflect a culture outside the United States

✓ ideas and observations from the narrator or speaker

✓ inferences made by drawing on a wide reading from world literature, such as

- dramas, plays, poetry, and short stories written by international authors
- stories that reflect an indigenous person's experience in another country

To analyze the point of view or cultural experience reflected in a work of literature from outside the United States, drawing on a wide reading of world literature, consider the following questions:

✓ What is the country of origin of the author and of the characters in the text? What details show that?

✓ What texts have you read previously from these nations or cultures? How does this help you analyze the cultural experience in this text?

✓ What is the author's, narrator's, or speaker's point of view? How do you know?

✓ How does this text use point of view to present a cultural experience different from that of the United States? How do you know?

✓ Is the narrator or speaker objective or unreliable? How does that affect the understanding of culture?

Please note that excerpts and passages in the StudySync® library and this workbook are intended as touchstones to generate interest in an author's work. The excerpts and passages do not substitute for the reading of entire texts, and StudySync® strongly recommends that students seek out and purchase the whole literary or informational work in order to experience it as the author intended. Links to online resellers are available in our digital library. In addition, complete works may be ordered through an authorized reseller by filling out and returning to StudySync® the order form enclosed in this workbook.

Reading & Writing Companion    55

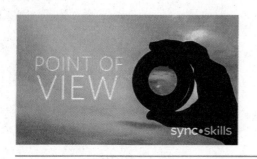

# Skill:
# Point of View

Reread paragraph 12 from "A Very Old Man with Enormous Wings." Then, using the Checklist on the previous page, answer the multiple-choice questions below.

## ↻ YOUR TURN

1. This question has two parts. First, answer Part A. Then, answer Part B.

   Part A: How has the family's point of view concerning the existence of the angel shifted by this stage of the story?

   ○ A. He is considered a holy creature to be treated with reverence.

   ○ B. He has become an annoyance.

   ○ C. He has made the people fearful.

   ○ D. He has brought joy and humor.

   Part B: Which of the following details BEST supports your answer from Part A?

   ○ A. "Pelayo threw a blanket over him and extended him the charity of letting him sleep in the shed."

   ○ B. "He could scarcely eat and his antiquarian eyes had also become so foggy that he went about bumping into posts."

   ○ C. "They would drive him out of the bedroom with a broom and a moment later find him in the kitchen."

   ○ D. "All he had left were the bare cannulae of his last feathers."

# Skill:
# Summarizing

Use the Checklist to analyze Summarizing in "A Very Old Man with Enormous Wings." Refer to the sample student annotation about Summarizing in the text.

## ••• CHECKLIST FOR SUMMARIZING

In order to determine how to write an objective summary of a text, note the following:

✓ how the theme or central idea develops over the course of the text

✓ how a theme emerges and is then shaped and refined by specific details

✓ answers to the basic questions *who, what, where, when, why,* and *how*

✓ avoidance of personal thoughts, judgments, or opinions

To provide an objective summary of a text, consider the following questions:

✓ What are the answers to basic *who, what, where, when, why,* and *how* questions in literature and works of nonfiction?

✓ What is the theme or central idea of the text?

✓ Does my summary include how the theme or central idea is developed over the course of the text?

✓ Does my summary demonstrate how that theme is shaped and refined by choosing only important details?

✓ Is my summary objective, or have I added my own thoughts, judgments, and personal opinions?

Please note that excerpts and passages in the StudySync® library and this workbook are intended as touchstones to generate interest in an author's work. The excerpts and passages do not substitute for the reading of entire texts, and StudySync® strongly recommends that students seek out and purchase the whole literary or informational work in order to experience it as the author intended. Links to online resellers are available in our digital library. In addition, complete works may be ordered through an authorized reseller by filling out and returning to StudySync® the order form enclosed in this workbook.

Reading & Writing
Companion

57

# Skill:
# Summarizing

Reread paragraph 13 of "A Very Old Man with Enormous Wings." Then, using the Checklist on the previous page, answer the multiple-choice questions below.

## ⟳ YOUR TURN

1. This question has two parts. First, answer Part A. Then, answer Part B.

   **Part A:** Which of the following is the BEST summary of the events in paragraph 13?

   ○ A. The angel survives the winter. He starts to grow new feathers and is very protective of them, hiding them so that people can't see them. He spends a lot of time hiding in the corner of the courtyard.

   ○ B. The angel survives the winter and flies away.

   ○ C. The angel survives the winter, grows new feathers, and flies away. The family is relieved but they shouldn't be because now they have no way to make more money.

   ○ D. The angel survives the winter and begins gaining strength. He grows new feathers and one day he flies away, to the relief of the family.

   **Part B:** Which of the following details are the MOST important for your summary from part A?

   ○ A. "large, stiff feathers began to grow on his wings"

   ○ B. "One morning Elisenda was cutting some bunches of onions for lunch"

   ○ C. "They were so clumsy that his fingernails opened a furrow in the vegetable patch"

   ○ D. "the feathers of a scarecrow, which looked more like another misfortune of decrepitude"

A VERY OLD MAN
WITH ENORMOUS WINGS

# Close Read

Reread "A Very Old Man with Enormous Wings." As you reread, complete the Skills Focus questions below. Then use your answers and annotations from the questions to help you complete the Write activity.

## ◎ SKILLS FOCUS

1. Summarize the short story, briefly and objectively.

2. Discuss how a particular cultural experience is reflected in this Colombian short story.

3. Determine the theme or central idea of the short story and analyze how it is shaped using two or three specific details.

4. García Márquez's short story reflects such source material as the myth of Icarus, the work of medieval theologians such as Thomas Aquinas (concerning angels), as well as the Catholicism of the people of South America. Research one of these allusions and analyze how the new representation uses the allusion for effect or to reveal a theme.

5. Discuss how the angel's arrival affects or guides the lives of the people in this village. Cite evidence from the text to support your ideas.

## ✎ WRITE

LITERARY ANALYSIS: García Márquez uses this work of magical realism to convey a social and moral point of view to the reader. What elements of the story are magical? What elements are realistic? How does the combination of magic and realism help convey a social and moral point of view in a way that other methods cannot? Use textual evidence and original analysis in your response.

Please note that excerpts and passages in the StudySync® library and this workbook are intended as touchstones to generate interest in an author's work. The excerpts and passages do not substitute for the reading of entire texts, and StudySync® strongly recommends that students seek out and purchase the whole literary or informational work in order to experience it as the author intended. Links to online resellers are available in our digital library. In addition, complete works may be ordered through an authorized reseller by filling out and returning to StudySync® the order form enclosed in this workbook.

Reading & Writing Companion    59

# The Nose

FICTION
Nikolai Gogol
1836

## Introduction

Nikolai Gogol (1809–1852) was one of the preeminent Russian writers of the 19th century. While he is a central figure of the natural school of Russian realism (a group whose members also included towering Russian authors like Turgenev and Dostoevsky), Gogol's work was also darkly humorous, surreal, and grotesque. In the city of St. Petersburg, Russia, in the early 1800s, a barber awakens. He slices into his morning roll and makes an unexpected discovery: inside the roll, a nose! What's more, he recognizes it as the nose of one of his customers—a bureaucrat named Kovalev. What ensues is an uproarious satire of Russian society, bureaucracy, and vanity, as the reader follows Kovalev on his journey to find his renegade nose.

# "Ivan Yakovlevitch was dumbfounded. He thought and thought, but did not know what to think."

I

1   ON 25 March an unusually strange event occurred in St. Petersburg. For that morning Barber Ivan Yakovlevitch, a dweller on the Vozkresensky Prospekt (his name is lost now—it no longer figures on a signboard bearing a portrait of a gentleman with a soaped cheek, and the words: "Also, Blood Let Here")—for that morning Barber Ivan Yakovlevitch awoke early, and caught the smell of newly baked bread. Raising himself a little, he perceived his wife (a most respectable dame, and one especially fond of coffee) to be just in the act of drawing newly baked rolls from the oven.

Portrait of Nikolai Gogol

2   "Prascovia Osipovna," he said, "I would rather not have any coffee for breakfast, but, instead, a hot roll and an onion,"—the truth being that he wanted both but knew it to be useless to ask for two things at once, as Prascovia Osipovna did not fancy such tricks.

3   "Oh, the fool shall have his bread," the dame reflected. "So much the better for me then, as I shall be able to drink a second lot of coffee."

4   And duly she threw on to the table a roll.

5   Ivan Yakovlevitch donned a jacket over his shirt for politeness' sake, and, seating himself at the table, poured out salt, got a couple of onions ready, took a knife into his hand, assumed an air of importance, and cut the roll asunder. Then he glanced into the roll's middle. To his intense surprise he saw something glimmering there. He probed it cautiously with the knife— then poked at it with a finger.

6   "Quite solid it is!" he muttered. "What in the world is it likely to be?"

7   He thrust in, this time, all his fingers, and pulled forth—a nose! His hands dropped to his sides for a moment. Then he rubbed his eyes hard. Then again he probed the thing. A nose! Sheerly a nose! Yes, and one familiar to him, somehow! Oh, horror spread upon his feature! Yet that horror was a trifle compared with his spouse's overmastering wrath.

8   "You brute!" she shouted frantically. "Where have you cut off that nose? You villain, you! You drunkard! Why, I'll go and report you to the police myself. The brigand, you! Three customers have told me already about your pulling at their noses as you shaved them till they could hardly stand it."

9   But Ivan Yakovlevitch was neither alive nor dead. This was the more the case because, sure enough, he had recognised the nose. It was the nose of Collegiate Assessor[1] Kovalev—no less: it was the nose of a gentleman whom he was accustomed to shave twice weekly, on each Wednesday and each Sunday!

10  "Stop, Prascovia Osipovna!" at length he said. "I'll wrap the thing in a clout, and lay it aside awhile, and take it away altogether later."

11  "But I won't hear of such a thing being done! As if I'm going to have a cut-off nose kicking about my room! Oh, you old stick! Maybe you can just strop a razor still; but soon you'll be no good at all for the rest of your work. You loafer, you wastrel, you bungler, you blockhead! Aye, I'll tell the police of you. Take it away, then. Take it away. Take it anywhere you like. Oh, that I'd never caught the smell of it!"

12  Ivan Yakovlevitch was dumbfounded. He thought and thought, but did not know what to think.

13  "The devil knows how it's happened," he said, scratching one ear. "You see, I don't know for certain whether I came home drunk last night or not. But certainly things look as though something out of the way happened then, for bread comes of baking, and a nose of something else altogether. Oh, I just can't make it out."

14  So he sat silent. At the thought that the police might find the nose at his place, and arrest him, he felt frantic. Yes, already he could see the red collar with the smart silver braiding—the sword! He shuddered from head to foot.

15  But at last he got out, and donned waistcoat and shoes, wrapped the nose in a clout, and departed amid Prascovia Osipovna's forcible objurgations.

---

1. **Collegiate Assessor** a position in the relative middle of the Table of Ranks, a hierarchy of social standing established in the early 18th century by Tsar Peter I (Peter the Great)

16　His one idea was to rid himself of the nose, and return quietly home—to do so either by throwing the nose into the gutter in front of the gates or by just letting it drop anywhere. Yet, unfortunately, he kept meeting friends, and they kept saying to him: "Where are you off to?" or "Whom have you arranged to shave at this early hour?" until seizure of a fitting moment became impossible. Once, true, he did succeed in dropping the thing, but no sooner had he done so than a constable pointed at him with his truncheon, and shouted: "Pick it up again! You've lost something," and he perforce had to take the nose into his possession once more, and stuff it into a pocket. Meanwhile his desperation grew in proportion as more and more booths and shops opened for business, and more and more people appeared in the street.

17　At last he decided that he would go to the Isaakievsky Bridge, and throw the thing, if he could, into the Neva. But here let me confess my fault in not having said more about Ivan Yakovlevitch himself, a man estimable in more respects than one.

18　Like every decent Russian tradesman, Ivan Yakovlevitch was a terrible tippler. Daily he shaved the chins of others[2], but always his own was unshorn, and his jacket (he never wore a top-coat) piebald—black, thickly studded with greyish, brownish-yellowish stains—and shiny of collar, and adorned with three pendent tufts of thread instead of buttons. But, with that, Ivan Yakovlevitch was a great cynic. Whenever Collegiate Assessor Kovalev was being shaved, and said to him, according to custom: "Ivan Yakovlevitch, your hands do smell!" he would retort: "But why should they smell?" and, when the Collegiate Assessor had replied: "Really I do not know, brother, but at all events they do," take a pinch of snuff[3], and soap the Collegiate Assessor upon cheek, and under nose, and behind ears, and around chin at his good will and pleasure.

19　So the worthy citizen stood on the Isaakievsky Bridge, and looked about him. Then, leaning over the parapet, he feigned to be trying to see if any fish were passing underneath. Then gently he cast forth the nose.

20　At once ten puds-weight seemed to have been lifted from his shoulders. Actually he smiled! But, instead of departing, next, to shave the chins of chinovniki, he bethought him of making for a certain establishment inscribed "Meals and Tea," that he might get there a glassful of punch.

21　Suddenly he sighted a constable standing at the end of the bridge, a constable of smart appearance, with long whiskers, a three-cornered hat, and a sword

---

2. **Daily he shaved the chins of others** around 1698, Peter the Great also imposed a "beard tax" because he didn't want Russian men to wear beards; he wanted them to look more "modern"

3. **snuff** chewing tobacco

complete. Oh, Ivan Yakovlevitch could have fainted! Then the constable, beckoning with a finger, cried:

22    "Nay, my good man. Come here."

23    Ivan Yaklovlevitch, knowing the proprieties, pulled off his cap at quite a distance away, advanced quickly, and said:

24    "I wish your Excellency the best of health."

25    "No, no! None of that 'your Excellency,' brother. Come and tell me what you have been doing on the bridge."

26    "Before God, sir, I was crossing it on my way to some customers when I peeped to see if there were any fish jumping."

27    "You lie, brother! You lie! You won't get out of it like that. Be so good as to answer me truthfully."

28    "Oh, twice a week in future I'll shave you for nothing. Aye, or even three times a week."

29    "No, no, friend. That is rubbish. Already I've got three barbers for the purpose, and all of them account it an honour. Now, tell me, I ask again, what you have just been doing?"

30    This made Ivan Yakovlevitch blanch, and——

31    Further events here become enshrouded in mist. What happened after that is unknown to all men.


      II

32    COLLEGIATE ASSESSOR KOVALEV also awoke early that morning. And when he had done so he made the "B-r-rh!" with his lips which he always did when he had been asleep—he himself could not have said why. Then he stretched himself, had handed to him a small mirror from the table near by, and set himself to inspect a pimple which had broken out on his nose the night before. But, to his unbounded astonishment, there was only a flat patch on his face where the nose should have been! Greatly alarmed, he called for water, washed, and rubbed his eyes hard with the towel. Yes, the nose indeed was gone! He prodded the spot with a hand—pinched himself to make sure that he was not still asleep. But no; he was not still sleeping. Then he leapt from the bed, and shook himself. No nose had he on him still! Finally, he bade his clothes be handed him, and set forth for the office of the Police Commissioner at his utmost speed.

33 Here let me add something which may enable the reader to perceive just what the Collegiate Assessor was like. Of course, it goes without saying that Collegiate Assessors who acquire the title with the help of academic diplomas cannot be compared with Collegiate Assessors who become Collegiate Assessors through service in the Caucasus, for the two species are wholly **distinct,** they are——Stay, though. Russia is so strange a country that, let one but say anything about any one Collegiate Assessor, and the rest, from Riga to Kamchatka, at once apply the remark to themselves—for all titles and all ranks it means the same thing. Now, Kovalev was a "Caucasian" Collegiate Assessor, and had, as yet, borne the title for two years only. Hence, unable ever to forget it, he sought the more to give himself dignity and weight by calling himself, in addition to "Collegiate Assessor," "Major."

34 "Look here, good woman," once he said to a shirts' vendor whom he met in the street, "come and see me at my home. I have my flat in Sadovaia Street. Ask merely, 'Is this where Major Kovalev lives?' Anyone will show you." Or, on meeting fashionable ladies, he would say: "My dear madam, ask for Major Kovalev's flat." So we too will call the Collegiate Assessor "Major."

35 Major Kovalev had a habit of daily promenading the Nevsky Prospekt in an extremely clean and well-starched shirt and collar, and in whiskers of the sort still observable on provincial surveyors, architects, regimental doctors, other officials, and all men who have round, red cheeks, and play a good hand at "Boston." Such whiskers run across the exact centre of the cheek—then head straight for the nose. Again, Major Kovalev always had on him a quantity of seals, both of seals engraved with coats of arms, and of seals inscribed "Wednesday," "Thursday," "Monday," and the rest. And, finally, Major Kovalev had come to live in St. Petersburg because of necessity. That is to say, he had come to live in St. Petersburg because he wished to obtain a post befitting his new title—whether a Vice-Governorship or, failing that, an Administratorship in a leading department. Nor was Major Kovalev altogether set against marriage. Merely he required that his bride should possess not less than two hundred thousand rubles in capital. The reader, therefore, can now judge how the Major was situated when he perceived that instead of a not unpresentable nose there was figuring on his face an extremely uncouth, and perfectly smooth and uniform patch.

36 Ill luck prescribed, that morning, that not a cab was visible throughout the street's whole length; so, huddling himself up in his cloak, and covering his face with a handkerchief (to make things look as though his nose were bleeding), he had to start upon his way on foot only.

37 "Perhaps this is only imagination?" he reflected. Presently he turned aside towards a restaurant (for he wished yet again to get a sight of himself in a mirror). "The nose can't have removed itself of sheer idiocy."

Please note that excerpts and passages in the StudySync® library and this workbook are intended as touchstones to generate interest in an author's work. The excerpts and passages do not substitute for the reading of entire texts, and StudySync® strongly recommends that students seek out and purchase the whole literary or informational work in order to experience it as the author intended. Links to online resellers are available in our digital library. In addition, complete works may be ordered through an authorized reseller by filling out and returning to StudySync® the order form enclosed in this workbook.

Reading & Writing Companion 65

38 Luckily no customers were present in the restaurant—merely some waiters were sweeping out the rooms, and rearranging the chairs, and others, sleepy-eyed fellows, were setting forth trayfuls of hot pastries. On chairs and tables last night's newspapers, coffee-stained, were strewn.

39 "Thank God that no one is here!" the Major reflected. "Now I can look at myself again."

40 He approached a mirror in some trepidation, and peeped therein. Then he spat.

41 "The devil only knows what this vileness means!" he muttered. "If even there had been something to take the nose's place! But, as it is, there's nothing there at all."

42 He bit his lips with vexation, and hurried out of the restaurant. No; as he went along he must look at no one, and smile at no one. Then he halted as though riveted to earth. For in front of the doors of a mansion he saw occur a phenomenon of which, simply, no explanation was possible. Before that mansion there stopped a carriage. And then a door of the carriage opened, and there leapt thence, huddling himself up, a uniformed gentleman, and that uniformed gentleman ran headlong up the mansion's entrance-steps, and disappeared within. And oh, Kovalev's horror and astonishment to perceive that the gentleman was none other than—his own nose! The unlooked-for spectacle made everything swim before his eyes. Scarcely, for a moment, could he even stand. Then, deciding that at all costs he must await the gentleman's return to the carriage, he remained where he was, shaking as though with fever. Sure enough, the Nose did return, two minutes later. It was clad in a gold-braided, high-collared uniform, buckskin breeches, and cockaded hat. And slung beside it there was a sword, and from the cockade on the hat it could be inferred that the Nose was purporting to pass for a State Councillor. It seemed now to be going to pay another visit somewhere. At all events it glanced about it, and then, shouting to the coachman, "Drive up here," re-entered the vehicle, and set forth.

43 Poor Kovalev felt almost demented. The astounding event left him utterly at a loss. For how could the nose which had been on his face but yesterday, and able then neither to drive nor to walk independently, now be going about in uniform?—He started in pursuit of the carriage, which, luckily, did not go far, and soon halted before the Gostiny Dvor.

44 Kovalev too hastened to the building, pushed through the line of old beggar-women with bandaged faces and apertures for eyes whom he had so often scorned, and entered. Only a few customers were present, but Kovalev felt so upset that for a while he could decide upon no course of action save to

scan every corner in the gentleman's pursuit. At last he sighted him again, standing before a counter, and, with face hidden altogether behind the uniform's stand-up collar, inspecting with absorbed attention some wares.

45 "How, even so, am I to approach it?" Kovalev reflected. "Everything about it, uniform, hat, and all, seems to show that it is a State Councillor now. Only the devil knows what is to be done!"

46 He started to cough in the Nose's vicinity, but the Nose did not change its position for a single moment.

47 "My good sir," at length Kovalev said, compelling himself to boldness, "my good sir, I——"

48 "What do you want?" And the Nose did then turn round.

49 "My good sir, I am in a difficulty. Yet somehow, I think, I think, that—well, I think that you ought to know your proper place better. All at once, you see, I find you—*where*? Do you not feel as I do about it?"

50 "Pardon me, but I cannot apprehend your meaning. Pray explain further."

51 "Yes, but how, I should like to know?" Kovalev thought to himself. Then, again taking courage, he went on:

52 "I am, you see—well, in point of fact, you see, I am a Major. Hence you will realise how unbecoming it is for me to have to walk about without a nose. Of course, a peddler of oranges on the Vozkresensky Bridge could sit there noseless well enough, but I myself am hoping soon to receive a——Hm, yes. Also, I have amongst my acquaintances several ladies of good houses (Madame Chektareva, wife of the State Councillor, for example), and you may judge for yourself what that alone signifies. Good sir"—Major Kovalev gave his shoulders a shrug—"I do not know whether you yourself (pardon me) consider conduct of this sort to be altogether in accordance with the rules of duty and honour, but at least you can understand that——"

53 "I understand nothing at all," the Nose broke in. "Explain yourself more satisfactorily."

54 "Good sir," Kovalev went on with a heightened sense of dignity, "the one who is at a loss to understand the other is I. But at least the immediate point should be plain, unless you are determined to have it otherwise. Merely—you are my own nose."

55 The Nose regarded the Major, and contracted its brows a little.

56 "My dear sir, you speak in error," was its reply. "I am just myself—myself separately. And in any case there cannot ever have existed a close relation between us, for, judging from the buttons of your undress uniform, your service is being performed in another department than my own."

57 And the Nose definitely turned away.

58 Kovalev stood dumbfounded. What to do, even what to think, he had not a notion.

59 Presently the agreeable swish of ladies' dresses began to be heard. Yes, an elderly, lace-bedecked dame was approaching, and, with her, a slender maiden in a white frock which outlined delightfully a trim figure, and, above it, a straw hat of a lightness as of pastry. Behind them there came, stopping every now and then to open a snuffbox, a tall, whiskered beau in quite a twelve-fold collar.

60 Kovalev moved a little nearer, pulled up the collar of his shirt, straightened the seals on his gold watch-chain, smiled, and directed special attention towards the slender lady as, swaying like a floweret in spring, she kept raising to her brows a little white hand with fingers almost of transparency. And Kovalev's smiles became broader still when peeping from under the hat he saw there to be an alabaster, rounded little chin, and part of a cheek flushed like an early rose. But all at once he recoiled as though scorched, for all at once he had remembered that he had not a nose on him, but nothing at all. So, with tears forcing themselves upwards, he wheeled about to tell the uniformed gentleman that he, the uniformed gentleman, was no State Councillor, but an impostor and a knave and a villain and the Major's own nose. But the Nose, behold, was gone! That very moment had it driven away to, **presumably**, pay another visit.

61 This drove Kovalev to the last pitch of desperation. He went back to the mansion, and stationed himself under its portico, in the hope that, by peering hither and thither, hither and thither, he might once more see the Nose appear. But, well though he remembered the Nose's cockaded hat and gold-braided uniform, he had failed at the time to note also its cloak, the colour of its horses, the make of its carriage, the look of the lackey seated behind, and the pattern of the lackey's livery. Besides, so many carriages were moving swiftly up and down the street that it would have been impossible to note them all, and equally so to have stopped any one of them. Meanwhile, as the day was fine and sunny, the Prospekt was thronged with pedestrians also—a whole kaleidoscopic stream of ladies was flowing along the pavements, from Police Headquarters to the Anitchkin Bridge. There one could descry an Aulic Councillor whom Kovalev knew well. A gentleman he was whom Kovalev always addressed as "Lieutenant-Colonel," and especially in the presence of

others. And there there went Yaryzhkin, Chief Clerk to the Senate, a crony who always rendered forfeit at "Boston" on playing an eight. And, lastly, a like "Major" with Kovalev, a like "Major" with an Assessorship acquired through Caucasian service, started to beckon to Kovalev with a finger!

62 "The devil take him!" was Kovalev's muttered comment. "Hi, cabman! Drive to the Police Commissioner's direct."

63 But just when he was entering the drozhki he added:

64 "No. Go by Ivanovskaia Street."

65 "Is the Commissioner in?" he asked on crossing the threshold.

66 "He is not," was the doorkeeper's reply. "He's gone this very moment."

67 "There's luck for you!"

68 "Aye," the doorkeeper went on. "Only just a moment ago he was off. If you'd been a bare half-minute sooner you'd have found him at home, maybe."

69 Still holding the handkerchief to his face, Kovalev returned to the cab, and cried wildly:

70 "Drive on!"

71 "Where to, though?" the cabman inquired.

72 "Oh, straight ahead!"

73 "'Straight ahead'? But the street divides here. To right, or to left?"

74 The question caused Kovalev to pause and recollect himself. In his situation he ought to make his next step an application to the Board of Discipline—not because the Board was directly connected with the police, but because its dispositions would be executed more speedily than in other departments. To seek satisfaction of the the actual department in which the Nose had declared itself to be serving would be sheerly unwise, since from the Nose's very replies it was clear that it was the sort of individual who held nothing sacred, and, in that event, might lie as unconsciously as it had lied in asserting itself never to have figured in its proprietor's company. Kovalev, therefore, decided to seek the Board of Discipline. But just as he was on the point of being driven thither there occurred to him the thought that the impostor and knave who had behaved so shamelessly during the late encounter might even now be using the time to get out of the city, and that in that case all further pursuit of the rogue would become vain, or at all events last for, God preserve us! a

full month. So at last, left only to the guidance of Providence, the Major resolved to make for a newspaper office, and publish a circumstantial description of the Nose in such good time that anyone meeting with the truant might at once be able either to restore it to him or to give information as to its whereabouts. So he not only directed the cabman to the newspaper office, but, all the way thither, prodded him in the back, and shouted: "Hurry up, you rascal! Hurry up, you rogue!" whilst the cabman intermittently responded: "Aye, barin," and nodded, and plucked at the reins of a steed as shaggy as a spaniel.

75     The moment that the drozhki halted Kovalev dashed, breathless, into a small reception-office. There, seated at a table, a grey-headed clerk in ancient jacket and pair of spectacles was, with pen tucked between lips, counting sums received in copper.

76     "Who here takes the advertisements?" Kovalev exclaimed as he entered. "A-ah! Good day to you."

77     "And my respects," the grey-headed clerk replied, raising his eyes for an instant, and then lowering them again to the spread out copper heaps.

78     "I want you to publish——"

79     "Pardon—one moment." And the clerk with one hand committed to paper a figure, and with a finger of the other hand shifted two accounts markers. Standing beside him with an advertisement in his hands, a footman in a laced coat, and sufficiently smart to seem to be in service in an aristocratic mansion, now thought well to display some knowingness.

80     "Sir," he said to the clerk, "I do assure you that the puppy is not worth eight grivni even. At all events I wouldn't give that much for it. Yet the countess loves it—yes, just loves it, by God! Anyone wanting it of her will have to pay a hundred rubles. Well, to tell the truth between you and me, people's tastes differ. Of course, if one's a sportsman one keeps a setter or a spaniel. And in that case don't you spare five hundred rubles, or even give a thousand, if the dog is a good one."

81     The worthy clerk listened with gravity, yet none the less accomplished a calculation of the number of letters in the advertisement brought. On either side there was a group of charwomen, shop assistants, doorkeepers, and the like. All had similar advertisements in their hands, with one of the documents to notify that a coachman of good character was about to be disengaged, and another one to advertise a koliaska imported from Paris in 1814, and only slightly used since, and another one a maid-servant of nineteen experienced in laundry work, but prepared also for other jobs, and another one a sound

drozhki save that a spring was lacking, and another one a grey-dappled, spirited horse of the age of seventeen, and another one some turnip and radish seed just received from London, and another one a country house with every amenity, stabling for two horses, and **sufficient** space for the laying out of a fine birch or spruce plantation, and another one some second-hand footwear, with, added, an invitation to attend the daily auction sale from eight o'clock to three. The room where the company thus stood gathered together was small, and its atmosphere confined; but this closeness, of course, Collegiate Assessor Kovalev never perceived, for, in addition to his face being muffled in a handkerchief, his nose was gone, and God only knew its present habitat!

82    "My dear sir," at last he said impatiently, "allow me to ask you something: it is a pressing matter."

83    "One moment, one moment! Two rubles, forty-three kopeks. Yes, presently. Sixty rubles, four kopeks."

84    With which the clerk threw the two advertisements concerned towards the group of charwomen and the rest, and turned to Kovalev.

85    "Well?" he said. "What do you want?"

86    "Your pardon," replied Kovalev, "but fraud and knavery has been done. I still cannot understand the affair, but wish to announce that anyone returning me the rascal shall receive an adequate reward."

87    "Your name, if you would be so good?"

88    "No, no. What can my name matter? I cannot tell it you. I know many acquaintances such as Madame Chektareva (wife of the State Councillor) and Pelagea Grigorievna Podtochina (wife of the Staff-Officer), and, the Lord preserve us, they would learn of the affair at once. So say just 'a Collegiate Assessor,' or, better, 'a gentleman ranking as Major.'"

89    "Has a household serf of yours absconded, then?"

90    "A household serf of mine? As though even a household serf would perpetrate such a crime as the present one! No, indeed! It is my nose that has absconded from me."

91    "Gospodin Nossov, Gospoding Nossov? Indeed a strange name, that![4] Then has this Gospodin Nossov robbed you of some money?"

---

4. **Indeed a strange name, that!:** *Noss* means "nose" in Russian, and *Gospodin* is equivalent to the English "Mr."

NOTES

92    "I said nose, not Nossov. You are making a mistake. There has disappeared, goodness knows whither, my nose, my own actual nose. Presumably it is trying to make a fool of me."

93    "But how could it so disappear? The matter has something about it which I do not fully understand."

94    "I cannot tell you the exact how. The point is that now the nose is driving about the city, and giving itself out for a State Councillor —wherefore I beg you to announce that anyone apprehending any such nose ought at once, in the shortest possible space of time, to return it to myself. Surely you can judge what it is for me meanwhile to be lacking such a conspicuous portion of my frame? For a nose is not like a toe which one can keep inside a boot, and hide the absence of if it is not there. Besides, every Thurdsay I am due to call upon Madame Chektareva (wife of the State Councillor): whilst Pelagea Grigorievna Podtochina (wife of the Staff-Officer, mother of a pretty daughter) also is one of my closest acquaintances. So, again, judge for yourself how I am situated at present. In such a condition as this I could not possibly present myself before the ladies named."

95    Upon that the clerk became thoughtful: the fact was clear from his tightly compressed lips alone.

96    "No," he said at length. "Insert such an announcement I cannot."

97    "But why not?"

98    "Because, you see, it might injure the paper's reputation. Imagine if everyone were to start proclaiming a disappearance of his nose! People would begin to say that, that—well, that we printed absurdities and false tales."

99    "But how is this matter a false tale? Nothing of the sort has it got about *it*."

100   "You think not; but only last week a similar case occurred. One day a chinovnik brought us an advertisement as you have done. The cost would have been only two rubles, seventy-three kopeks, for all that it seemed to signify was the running away of a poodle. Yet what was it, do you think, in reality? Why, the thing turned out to be a libel, and the 'poodle' in question a cashier—of what department precisely I do not know."

101   "Yes, but here am I advertising not about a poodle, but about my own nose, which, surely, is, for all intents and purposes, myself?"

102   "All the same, I cannot insert the advertisement."

103   "Even when actually I have lost my own nose!"

104   "The fact that your nose is gone is a matter for a doctor. There are doctors, I have heard, who can fit one out with any sort of nose one likes. I take it that by nature you are a wag, and like playing jokes in public."

105   "That is not so. I swear it as God is holy. In fact, as things have gone so far, I will let you see for yourself."

106   "Why trouble?" Here the clerk took some snuff before adding with, nevertheless, a certain movement of curiosity: "However, if it really won't trouble you at all, a sight of the spot would gratify me."

107   The Collegiate Assessor removed the handkerchief.

108   "Strange indeed! Very strange indeed!" the clerk exclaimed. "And the patch is as uniform as a newly fried pancake, almost unbelievably uniform."

109   "So you will dispute what I say no longer? Then surely you cannot but put the announcement into print. I shall be extremely grateful to you, and glad that the present occasion has given me such a pleasure as the making of your acquaintance"—whence it will be seen that for once the Major had decided to climb down.

110   "To print what you want is nothing much," the clerk replied. "Yet frankly I cannot see how you are going to benefit from the step. I would suggest, rather, that you commission a skilled writer to compose an article describing this as a rare product of nature, and have the article published in *The Northern Bee*" (here the clerk took more snuff), "either for the instruction of our young" (the clerk wiped his nose for a finish) "or as a matter of general interest."

111   This again depressed the Collegiate Assessor: and even though, on his eyes happening to fall upon a copy of the newspaper, and reach the column assigned to theatrical news, and encounter the name of a beautiful actress, so that he almost broke into a smile, and a hand began to finger a pocket for a Treasury note (since he held that only stalls were seats befitting Majors and so forth)—although all this was so, there again recurred to him the thought of the nose, and everything again became spoilt.

112   Even the clerk seemed touched with the awkwardness of Kovalev's plight, and wishful to lighten with a few sympathetic words the Collegiate Assessor's depression.

113   "I am sorry indeed that this has befallen," he said. "Should you care for a pinch of this? Snuff can dissipate both headache and low spirits. Nay, it is good for haemorrhoids as well."

114　And he proffered his box-deftly, as he did so, folding back underneath it the lid depicting a lady in a hat.

115　Kovalev lost his last shred of patience at the thoughtless act, and said heatedly:

116　"How you can think fit thus to jest I cannot imagine. For surely you perceive me no longer to be in possession of a means of sniffing? Oh, you and your snuff can go to hell! Even the sight of it is more than I can bear. I should say the same even if you were offering me, not wretched birch bark, but real rappee."

117　Greatly incensed, he rushed out of the office, and made for the ward police inspector's residence. Unfortunately he arrived at the very moment when the inspector, after a yawn and a stretch, was reflecting: "Now for two hours' sleep!" In short, the Collegiate Assessor's visit chanced to be exceedingly ill-timed. Incidentally, the inspector, though a great patron of manufacturers and the arts, preferred still more a Treasury note.

118　"That's the thing!" he frequently would say. "It's a thing which can't be beaten anywhere, for it wants nothing at all to eat, and it takes up very little room, and it fits easily to the pocket, and it doesn't break in pieces if it happens to be dropped."

119　So the inspector received Kovalev very drily, and intimated that just after dinner was not the best moment for beginning an inquiry—nature had ordained that one should rest after food (which showed the Collegiate Assessor that at least the inspector had some knowledge of sages' old saws), and that in any case no one would purloin the nose of a *really* respectable man.

120　Yes, the inspector gave it Kovalev between the eyes. And as it should be added that Kovalev was extremely sensitive where his title or his dignity was concerned (though he readily pardoned anything said against himself personally, and even held, with regard to stage plays, that, whilst Staff-Officers should not be assailed, officers of lesser rank might be referred to), the police inspector's reception so took him aback that, in a dignified way, and with hands set apart a little, he nodded, remarked: "After your insulting observations there is nothing which I wish to add," and betook himself away again.

121　He reached home scarcely hearing his own footsteps. Dusk had fallen, and, after the unsuccessful questings, his flat looked truly dreary. As he entered the hall he perceived Ivan, his valet, to be lying on his back on the stained old leathern divan, and spitting at the ceiling with not a little skill as regards successively hitting the same spot. The man's coolness rearoused Kovalev's ire, and, smacking him over the head with his hat, he shouted:

122 "You utter pig! You do nothing but play the fool." Leaping up, Ivan hastened to take his master's cloak.

123 The tired and despondent Major then sought his sitting-room, threw himself into an easy-chair, sighed, and said to himself:

124 "My God, my God! why has this misfortune come upon me? Even loss of hands or feet would have been better, for a man without a nose is the devil knows what—a bird, but not a bird, a citizen, but not a citizen, a thing just to be thrown out of window. It would have been better, too, to have had my nose cut off in action, or in a duel, or through my own act: whereas here is the nose gone with nothing to show for it—uselessly—for not a groat's profit!— No, though," he added after thought, "it's not likely that the nose is gone for good: it's not likely at all. And quite probably I am dreaming all this, or am fuddled. It may be that when I came home yesterday I drank the vodka with which I rub my chin after shaving instead of water—snatched up the stuff because that fool Ivan was not there to receive me."

125 So he sought to ascertain whether he might not be drunk by pinching himself till he fairly yelled. Then, certain, because of the pain, that he was acting and living in waking life, he approached the mirror with diffidence, and once more scanned himself with a sort of inward hope that the nose might by this time be showing as restored. But the result was merely that he recoiled and muttered:

126 "What an absurd spectacle still!"

127 Ah, it all passed his understanding! If only a button, or a silver spoon, or a watch, or some such article were gone, rather than that anything had disappeared like this—for no reason, and in his very flat! Eventually, having once more reviewed the circumstances, he reached the final conclusion that he should most nearly hit the truth in supposing Madame Podtochina (wife of the Staff-Officer, of course—the lady who wanted him to become her daughter's husband) to have been the prime agent in the affair. True, he had always liked dangling in the daughter's wake, but also he had always fought shy of really coming down to business. Even when the Staff-Officer's lady had said point blank that she desired him to become her son-in-law he had put her off with his compliments, and replied that the daughter was still too young, and himself due yet to perform five years service, and aged only forty-two. Yes, the truth must be that out of revenge the Staff-Officer's wife had resolved to ruin him, and hired a band of witches for the purpose, seeing that the nose could not **conceivably** have been cut off—no one had entered his private

room lately, and, after being shaved by Ivan Yakovlevitch on the Wednesday, he had the nose intact, he knew and remembered well, throughout both the rest of the Wednesday and the day following. Also, if the nose had been cut off, pain would have resulted, and also a wound, and the place could not have healed so quickly, and become of the uniformity of a pancake.

128    Next, the Major made his plans. Either he would sue the Staff-Officer's lady in legal form or he would pay her a surprise visit, and catch her in a trap. Then the foregoing reflections were cut short by a glimmer showing through the chink of the door—a sign that Ivan had just lit a candle in the hall: and presently Ivan himself appeared, carrying the candle in front of him, and throwing the room into such clear radiance that Kovalev had hastily to snatch up the handkerchief again, and once more cover the place where the nose had been but yesterday, lest the stupid fellow should be led to stand gaping at the monstrosity on his master's features.

129    Ivan had just returned to his cupboard when an unfamiliar voice in the hall inquired:

130    "Is this where Collegiate Assessor Kovalev lives?"

131    "It is," Kovalev shouted, leaping to his feet, and flinging wide the door. "Come in, will you?"

132    Upon which there entered a police-officer of smart exterior, with whiskers neither light nor dark, and cheeks nicely plump. As a matter of fact, he was the police-officer whom Ivan Yakovlevitch had met at the end of the Isaakievsky Bridge.

133    "I beg your pardon, sir," he said, "but have you lost your nose?"

134    "I have—just so."

135    "Then the nose is found."

136    "What?" For a moment or two joy deprived Major Kovalev of further speech. All that he could do was to stand staring, open-eyed, at the officer's plump lips and cheeks, and at the tremulant beams which the candlelight kept throwing over them. "Then how did it come about?"

137    "Well, by the merest chance the nose was found beside a roadway. Already it had entered a stage-coach, and was about to leave for Riga with a passport made out in the name of a certain chinovnik. And, curiously enough, I myself, at first, took it to be a gentleman. Luckily, though, I had my eyeglasses on me. Soon, therefore, I perceived the 'gentleman' to be no more than a nose. Such

is my shortness of sight, you know, that even now, though I see you standing there before me, and see that you have a face, I cannot distinguish on that face the nose, the chin, or anything else. My mother-in-law (my wife's mother) too cannot easily distinguish details."

138 Kovalev felt almost beside himself.

139 "Where is the nose now?" cried he. "Where, I ask? Let me go to it at once."

140 "Do not trouble, sir. Knowing how greatly you stand in need of it, I have it with me. It is a curious fact, too, that the chief agent in the affair has been a rascal of a barber who lives on the Vozkresensky Prospekt, and now is sitting at the police station. For long past I had suspected him of drunkenness and theft, and only three days ago he took away from a shop a button-card. Well, you will find your nose to be as before."

141 And the officer delved into a pocket, and drew thence the nose, wrapped in paper.

142 "Yes, that's the nose all right!" Kovalev shouted. "It's the nose precisely! Will you join me in a cup of tea?"

143 "I should have accounted it indeed a pleasure if I had been able, but, unfortunately, I have to go straight on to the penitentiary. Provisions, sir, have risen greatly in price. And living with me I have not only my family, but my mother-in-law (my wife's mother). Yet the eldest of my children gives me much hope. He is a clever lad. The only thing is that I have not the means for his proper education."

144 When the officer was gone the Collegiate Assessor sat plunged in vagueness, plunged in inability to see or to feel, so greatly was he upset with joy. Only after a while did he with care take the thus recovered nose in cupped hands, and again examine it attentively.

145 "It, undoubtedly. It, precisely," he said at length. "Yes, and it even has on it the pimple to the left which broke out on me yesterday."

146 Sheerly he laughed in his delight.

147 But nothing lasts long in this world. Even joy grows less lively the next moment. And a moment later, again, it weakens further. And at last it remerges insensibly with the normal mood, even as the ripple from a pebble's impact becomes remerged with the smooth surface of the water at large. So Kovalev relapsed into thought again. For by now he had realised that even yet the affair was

not wholly ended, seeing that, though retrieved, the nose needed to be re-stuck.

148 "What if it should fail so to stick!"

149 The bare question thus posed turned the Major pale.

150 Feeling, somehow, very nervous, he drew the mirror closer to him, lest he should fit the nose awry. His hands were trembling as gently, very carefully he lifted the nose in place. But, oh, horrors, it would not *remain* in place! He held it to his lips, warmed it with his breath, and again lifted it to the patch between his cheeks—only to find, as before, that it would not retain its position.

151 "Come, come, fool!" said he. "Stop where you are, I tell you."

152 But the nose, obstinately wooden, fell upon the table with a strange sound as of a cork, whilst the Major's face became convulsed.

153 "Surely it is not too large now?" he reflected in terror. Yet as often as he raised it towards its proper position the new attempt proved as vain as the last.

154 Loudly he shouted for Ivan, and sent for a doctor who occupied a flat (a better one than the Major's) on the first floor. The doctor was a fine-looking man with splendid, coal-black whiskers. Possessed of a healthy, comely wife, he ate some raw apples every morning, and kept his mouth extraordinarily clean—rinsed it out, each morning, for three-quarters of an hour, and polished its teeth with five different sorts of brushes. At once he answered Kovalev's summons, and, after asking how long ago the calamity had happened, tilted the Major's chin, and rapped the vacant site with a thumb until at last the Major wrenched his head away, and, in doing so, struck it sharply against the wall behind. This, the doctor said, was nothing; and after advising him to stand a little farther from the wall, and bidding him incline his head to the right, he once more rapped the vacant patch before, after bidding him incline his head to the left, dealing him, with a "Hm!" such a thumb-dig as left the Major standing like a horse which is having its teeth examined.

155 The doctor, that done, shook his head.

156 "The thing is not feasible," he pronounced. "You had better remain as you are rather than go farther and fare worse. Of course, I *could* stick it on again—I could do that for you in a moment; but at the same time I would assure you that your plight will only become worse as the result."

157 "Never mind," Kovalev replied. "Stick it on again, pray. How can I continue without a nose? Besides, things could not possibly be worse than they are

now. At present they are the devil himself. Where can I show this caricature of a face? My circle of acquaintances is a large one: this very night I am due in two houses, for I know a great many people like Madame Chektareva (wife of the State Councillor), Madame Podtochina (wife of the Staff-Officer), and others. Of course, though, I shall have nothing further to do with Madame Podtochina (except through the police) after her present proceedings. Yes," persuasively he went on, "I beg of you to do me the favour requested. Surely there are means of doing it permanently? Stick it on in any sort of a fashion— at all events so that it will hold fast, even if not becomingly. And then, when risky moments occur, I might even support it gently with my hand, and likewise dance no more—anything to avoid fresh injury through an unguarded movement. For the rest, you may feel assured that I shall show you my gratitude for this visit so far as ever my means will permit."

158 "Believe me," the doctor replied, neither too loudly nor too softly, but just with incisiveness and magnetic "when I say that I never attend patients for money. To do that would be contrary alike to my rules and to my art. When I accept a fee for a visit I accept it only lest I offend through a refusal. Again I say—this time on my honour, as you will not believe my plain word—that, though I could easily re-affix your nose, the proceeding would make things worse, far worse, for you. It would be better for you to trust merely to the action of nature. Wash often in cold water, and I assure you that you will be as healthy without a nose as with one. This nose here I should advise you to put into a jar of spirit: or, better still, to steep in two tablespoonfuls of stale vodka and strong vinegar. Then you will be able to get a good sum for it. Indeed, I myself will take the thing if you consider it of no value."

159 "No, no!" shouted the distracted Major. "Not on any account will I sell it. I would rather it were lost again."

160 "Oh, I beg your pardon." And the doctor bowed. "My only idea had been to serve you. What is it you want? Well, you have seen me do what I could."

161 And majestically he withdrew. Kovalev, meanwhile, had never once looked at his face. In his distraction he had noticed nothing beyond a pair of snowy cuffs projecting from black sleeves.

162 He decided, next, that, before lodging a plea next day, he would write and request the Staff-Officer's lady to restore him his nose without publicity. His letter ran as follows:

163 DEAR MADAME ALEXANDRA GRIGORIEVNA, I am at a loss to understand your strange conduct. At least, however, you may rest assured that you will benefit nothing by it, and that it will in no way further force me to marry your daughter. Believe me, I am now aware of all the circumstances connected

with my nose, and know that you alone have been the prime agent in them. The nose's sudden disappearance, its subsequent gaddings about, its masqueradings as, firstly, a chinovnik and, secondly, itself—all these have come of witchcraft practised either by you or by adepts in pursuits of a refinement equal to your own. This being so, I consider it my duty herewith to warn you that if the nose should not this very day reassume its correct position, I shall be forced to have resort to the law's protection and defence. With all respect, I have the honour to remain your very humble servant, PLATON KOVALEV.

164    "MY DEAR SIR," wrote the lady in return, "your letter has greatly surprised me, and I will say frankly that I had not expected it, and least of all its unjust reproaches. I assure you that I have never at any time allowed the chinovnik whom you mention to enter my house—either masquerading or as himself. True, I have received calls from Philip Ivanovitch Potanchikov, who, as you know, is seeking my daughter's hand, and, besides, is a man steady and upright, as well as learned; but never, even so, have I given him reason to hope. You speak, too, of a nose. If that means that I seem to you to have desired to leave you with a nose and nothing else, that is to say, to return you a direct refusal of my daughter's hand, I am astonished at your words, for, as you cannot but be aware, my inclination is quite otherwise. So now, if still you wish for a formal betrothal to my daughter, I will readily, I do assure you, satisfy your desire, which all along has been, in the most lively manner, my own also. In hopes of that, I remain yours sincerely, ALEXANDRA PODTOCHINA.

165    "No, no!" Kovalev exclaimed, after reading the missive. "She, at least, is not guilty. Oh, certainly not! No one who had committed such a crime could write such a letter." The Collegiate Assessor was the more expert in such matters because more than once he had been sent to the Caucasus to institute prosecutions. "Then by what sequence of chances has the affair happened? Only the devil could say!"

166    His hands fell in bewilderment.

167    It had not been long before news of the strange occurrence had spread through the capital. And, of course, it received additions with the progress of time. Everyone's mind was, at that period, bent upon the marvellous. Recently experiments with the action of magnetism had occupied public attention, and the history of the dancing chairs of Koniushennaia Street also was fresh. So no one could wonder when it began to be said that the nose of Collegiate Assessor Kovalev could be seen promenading the Nevski Prospekt at three o'clock, or when a crowd of curious sightseers gathered there. Next, someone declared that the nose, rather, could be beheld at Junker's store, and the throng which surged thither became so massed as to necessitate a summons

to the police. Meanwhile a speculator of highly respectable aspect and whiskers who sold stale cakes at the entrance to a theatre knocked together some stout wooden benches, and invited the curious to stand upon them for eighty kopeks each; whilst a retired colonel who came out early to see the show, and penetrated the crowd only with great difficulty, was disgusted when in the window of the store he beheld, not a nose, but merely an ordinary woollen waistcoat flanked by the selfsame lithograph of a girl pulling up a stocking, whilst a dandy with cutaway waistcoat and receding chin peeped at her from behind a tree, which had hung there for ten years past.

168 "Dear me!" irritably he exclaimed. "How come people so to excite themselves about stupid, improbable reports?"

169 Next, word had it that the nose was walking, not on the Nevski Prospekt, but in the Taurida Park, and, in fact, had been in the habit of doing so for a long while past, so that even in the days when Khozrev Mirza had lived near there he had been greatly astonished at the freak of nature. This led students to repair thither from the College of Medicine, and a certain eminent, respected lady to write and ask the Warden of the Park to show her children the phenomenon, and, if possible, add to the demonstration a lesson of edifying and instructive tenor.

170 Naturally, these events greatly pleased also gentlemen who frequented routs, since those gentlemen wished to entertain the ladies, and their resources had become exhausted. Only a few solid, worthy persons deprecated it all. One such person even said, in his disgust, that comprehend how foolish inventions of the sort could circulate in such an enlightened age he could not—that, in fact, he was surprised that the Government had not turned its attention to the matter. From which utterance it will be seen that the person in question was one of those who would have dragged the Government into anything on earth, including even their daily quarrels with their wives.

171 Next——

172 But again events here become enshrouded in mist. What happened after that is unknown to all men.

III

173 FARCE really does occur in this world, and, sometimes, farce altogether without an element of probability. Thus, the nose which lately had gone about as a State Councillor, and stirred all the city, suddenly reoccupied its proper place (between the two cheeks of Major Kovalev) as though nothing at all had happened. The date was 7 April, and when, that morning, the major awoke as usual, and, as usual, threw a despairing glance at the mirror, he this time,

beheld before him, what?—why, the nose again! Instantly he took hold of it. Yes, the nose, the nose precisely! "Aha!" he shouted, and, in his joy, might have executed a trepak about the room in bare feet had not Ivan's entry suddenly checked him. Then he had himself furnished with materials for washing, washed, and glanced at the mirror again. Oh, the nose was there still! So next he rubbed it vigorously with the towel. Ah, still it was there, the same as ever!

174    "Look, Ivan," he said. "Surely there is a pimple on my nose?" But meanwhile he was thinking: "What if he should reply: 'You are wrong, sir. Not only is there not a pimple to be seen, but not even a nose'?"

175    However, all that Ivan said was:

176    "Not a pimple, sir, that isn't. The nose is clear all over."

177    "Good!" the Major reflected, and snapped his fingers. At the same moment Barber Ivan Yakovlevitch peeped round the door. He did so as timidly as a cat which has just been whipped for stealing cream.

178    "Tell me first whether your hands are clean?" the Major cried.

179    "They are, sir."

180    "You lie, I'll be bound."

181    "By God, sir, I do not!"

182    "Then go carefully."

183    As soon as Kovalev had seated himself in position Ivan Yakovlevitch vested him in a sheet, and plied brush upon chin and a portion of a cheek until they looked like the blanc mange served on tradesmen's namedays.

184    "Ah, you!" Here Ivan Yakovlevitch glanced at the nose. Then he bent his head askew, and contemplated the nose from a position on the flank. "It looks right enough," finally he commented, but eyed the member for quite a little while longer before carefully, so gently as almost to pass the imagination, he lifted two fingers towards it, in order to grasp its tip—such always being his procedure.

185    "Come, come! Do mind!" came in a shout from Kovalev. Ivan Yakovlevitch let fall his hands, and stood disconcerted, dismayed as he had never been before. But at last he started scratching the razor lightly under the chin, and, despite the unhandiness and difficulty of shaving in that quarter without also grasping the organ of smell, contrived, with the aid of a thumb planted firmly

upon the cheek and the lower gum, to overcome all obstacles, and bring the shave to a finish.

186 Everything thus ready, Kovalev dressed, called a cab, and set out for the restaurant. He had not crossed the threshold before he shouted: "Waiter! A cup of chocolate!" Then he sought a mirror, and looked at himself. The nose was still in place! He turned round in cheerful mood, and, with eyes contracted slightly, bestowed a bold, satirical scrutiny upon two military men, one of the noses on whom was no larger than a waistcoat button. Next, he sought the chancery of the department where he was **agitating** to obtain a Vice-Governorship (or, failing that, an Administratorship), and, whilst passing through the reception vestibule, again surveyed himself in a mirror. As much in place as ever the nose was!

187 Next, he went to call upon a brother Collegiate Assessor, a brother "Major." This colleague of his was a great satirist, but Kovalev always met his quarrelsome remarks merely with: "Ah, you! I know you, and know what a wag you are."

188 Whilst proceeding thither he reflected:

189 "At least, if the Major doesn't burst into laughter on seeing me, I shall know for certain that all is in order again."

190 And this turned out to be so, for the colleague said nothing at all on the subject.

191 "Splendid, damn it all!" was Kovalev's inward comment.

192 In the street, on leaving the colleague's, he met Madame Podtochina, and also Madame Podtochina's daughter. Bowing to them, he was received with nothing but joyous exclamations. Clearly all had been fancy, no harm had been done. So not only did he talk quite a while to the ladies, but he took special care, as he did so, to produce his snuffbox, and deliberately plug his nose at both entrances. Meanwhile inwardly he said:

193 "There now, good ladies! There now, you couple of hens! I'm not going to marry the daughter, though. All this is just—*par amour*, allow me."

194 And from that time onwards Major Kovalev gadded about the same as before. He walked on the Nevski Prospekt, and he visited theatres, and he showed himself everywhere. And always the nose accompanied him the same as before, and evinced no signs of again purposing a departure. Great was his good humour, replete was he with smiles, intent was he upon pursuit of fair ladies. Once, it was noted, he even halted before a counter of the Gostini

Dvor, and there purchased the riband of an order. Why precisely he did so is not known, for of no order was he a knight.

195　To think of such an affair happening in this our vast empire's northern capital! Yet general opinion decided that the affair had about it much of the improbable. Leaving out of the question the nose's strange, unnatural removal, and its subsequent appearance as a State Councillor, how came Kovalev not to know that one ought not to advertise for a nose through a newspaper? Not that I say this because I consider newspaper charges for announcements excessive. No, that is nothing, and I do not belong to the number of the mean. I say it because such a proceeding would have been *gauche*, derogatory, not the thing. And how came the nose into the baked roll? And what of Ivan Yakovlevitch? Oh, I cannot understand these points—absolutely I cannot. And the strangest, most unintelligible fact of all is that authors actually can select such occurrences for their subject! I confess this too to pass my comprehension, to——But no; I will say just that I do not understand it. In the first place, a course of the sort never benefits the country. And in the second place—in the second place, a course of the sort never benefits anything at all. I cannot divine the use of it.

196　Yet, even considering these things; even conceding this, that, and the other (for where are not incongruities found at times?) there may have, after all, been something in the affair. For no matter what folk say to the contrary, such affairs do happen in this world—rarely of course, yet none the less really.

## ✎ WRITE

LITERARY ANALYSIS: Nikolai Gogol's absurdist satire, "The Nose," is a forerunner of the genre known as magical realism. In what ways does Gogol's story of Major Kovalev reflect the traits of magical realism while putting forth a particular point of view of Russian society? Incorporate textual evidence that supports your claim.

# A Quilt of a Country

INFORMATIONAL TEXT
Anna Quindlen
2001

# Introduction

A nna Quindlen (b. 1952) is a decorated American journalist and author. She is a bestselling author of nine novels, three of which were made into movies. Anna also won the Pulitzer Prize for Commentary in 1992 for her op-ed column in the *New York Times*. "A Quilt of a Country" was written mere weeks after the September 11 terrorist attacks that devastated Americans. Quindlen's thoughts about America, especially in the wake of terrorism and fear, are poignant and personal since New York is her home. She dissects her homeland to its core, evaluating equality and tolerance—or lack thereof—in the contemporary American landscape.

# "America is an improbable idea. A mongrel nation built of ever-changing disparate parts . . ."

**Skill: Figurative Language**

*Two metaphors: 1) a quilt is many different pieces of fabric put together to make a whole blanket; 2) a mongrel is a mix of different breeds. Different people from many backgrounds together form the nation.*

1   America is an improbable idea. A mongrel[1] nation built of ever-changing **disparate** parts, it is held together by a notion, the notion that all men are created equal, though everyone knows that most men consider themselves better than someone. "Of all the nations in the world, the United States was built in nobody's image," the historian Daniel Boorstin wrote. That's because it was built of bits and pieces that seem discordant, like the crazy quilts that have been one of its great folk-art forms, velvet and calico and checks and brocades. Out of many, one. That is the ideal.

2   The reality is often quite different, a great national striving consisting frequently of failure. Many of the oft-told stories of the most pluralistic nation on earth are stories not of tolerance, but of **bigotry**. Slavery and sweatshops, the burning of crosses and the ostracism of the other. Children learn in social-studies class and in the news of the lynching of blacks, the denial of rights to women, the murders of gay men. It is difficult to know how to convince them that this amounts to "crown thy good with brotherhood," that amid all the failures is something spectacularly successful. Perhaps they understand it at this moment, when enormous tragedy, as it so often does, demands a time of reflection on enormous blessings.

3   This is a nation founded on a conundrum[2], what Mario Cuomo has characterized as "community added to individualism." These two are our defining ideals; they are also in constant conflict. Historians today bemoan the ascendancy of a kind of prideful apartheid[3] in America, saying that the clinging to ethnicity, in background and custom, has undermined the concept of unity. These historians must have forgotten the past, or have gilded it. The New York of my children is no more Balkanized[4], probably less so, than the Philadelphia of my father, in which Jewish boys would walk several blocks out

---

1. **mongrel**  of mixed descent; crossbred (often pejorative)
2. **conundrum**  a confusing or difficult puzzle or problem
3. **apartheid**  an institutionally enforced policy of racial separation, most commonly in reference to South Africa from after World War II until the 1990s
4. **Balkanized**  separated into small and mutually hostile parts; the reference is derived from the countries of the Balkan region of southeastern Europe leading up to and after Yugoslavian unification

of their way to avoid the Irish divide of Chester Avenue. (I was the product of a mixed marriage, across barely bridgeable lines: an Italian girl, an Irish boy. How quaint it seems now, how incendiary then.) The Brooklyn of Francie Nolan's famous tree, the Newark of which Portnoy complained, even the uninflected WASP suburbs of Cheever's characters: they are ghettos, pure and simple. Do the Cambodians and the Mexicans in California coexist less easily today than did the Irish and Italians of Massachusetts a century ago? You know the answer.

4   What is the point of this splintered whole? What is the point of a nation in which Arab cabbies chauffeur Jewish passengers through the streets of New York—and in which Jewish cabbies chauffeur Arab passengers, too, and yet speak in theory of hatred, one for the other? What is the point of a nation in which one part seems to be always on the verge of fisticuffs with another, blacks and whites, gays and straights, left and right, Pole and Chinese and Puerto Rican and Slovenian? Other countries with such divisions have in fact divided into new nations with new names, but not this one, impossibly interwoven even in its hostilities.

5   Once these disparate parts were held together by a common enemy, by the fault lines of world wars and the electrified fence of communism. With the end of the cold war there was the creeping concern that without a focus for hatred and distrust, a sense of national identity would evaporate, that the left side of the hyphen—African-American, Mexican-American, Irish-American—would overwhelm the right. And slow-growing domestic traumas like economic unrest and increasing crime seemed more likely to emphasize division than community. Today the citizens of the United States have come together once more because of armed conflict and enemy attack. Terrorism has led to devastation—and unity.

6   Yet even in 1994, the overwhelming majority of those surveyed by the National Opinion Research Center agreed with this statement: "The U.S. is a unique country that stands for something special in the world." One of the things that it stands for is this vexing notion that a great nation can consist entirely of refugees from other nations, that people of different, even warring religions and cultures can live, if not side by side, than on either side of the country's Chester Avenues. Faced with this diversity there is little point in trying to isolate anything remotely resembling a national character, but there are two strains of behavior that, however tenuously, **abet** the concept of unity.

7   There is that Calvinist[5] undercurrent in the American psyche that loves the difficult, the demanding, that sees mastering the impossible, whether it be

Skill: Word Patterns and Relationships

*I know the noun* splinter, *like a splinter of wood in my finger. I see that* splintered *here is an adjective describing* whole. *A splintered nation is broken up in some way, in this case ethnically.*

Skill: Word Patterns and Relationships

*The verb* vex *means "to cause distress." The addition of* -ing *makes it an adjective modifying* notion, *or idea. The author uses* vexing *sarcastically, since refugees living peacefully should not cause distress.*

---

5. **Calvinist** referring to the Reform tradition of Protestant Christianity established by French religious reformer John Calvin (1509–1564)

Copyright © BookheadEd Learning, LLC

prairie or subway, as a test of character, and so glories in the struggle of this fractured **coalescing**. And there is a grudging fairness among the citizens of the United States that eventually leads most to admit that, no matter what the English-only advocates try to suggest, the new immigrants are not so different from our own parents or grandparents. Leonel Castillo, former director of the Immigration and Naturalization Service and himself the grandson of Mexican immigrants, once told the writer Studs Terkel proudly, "The old neighborhood Ma-Pa stores are still around. They are not Italian or Jewish or Eastern European any more. Ma and Pa are now Korean, Vietnamese, Iraqi, Jordanian, Latin American. They live in the store. They work seven days a week. Their kids are doing well in school. They're making it. Sound familiar?"

8　Tolerance is the word used most often when this kind of coexistence succeeds, but tolerance is a vanilla-pudding word, standing for little more than the allowance of letting others live unremarked and unmolested. Pride seems excessive, given the American willingness to endlessly complain about them, them being whoever is new, different, unknown or currently under suspicion. But patriotism is partly taking pride in this unlikely ability to throw all of us together in a country that across its length and breadth is as different as a dozen countries, and still be able to call it by one name. When photographs of the faces of all those who died in the World Trade Center destruction are assembled in one place, it will be possible to trace in the skin color, the shape of the eyes and the noses, the texture of the hair, a map of the world. These are the representatives of a mongrel nation that somehow, at times like this, has one spirit. Like many improbable ideas, when it actually works, it's a wonder.

Skill: Arguments and Claims

*Repeating improbable reinforces the idea introduced in paragraph 1, that America is an "improbable idea." Quindlen reinforces her claim that an improbable idea can work: America can have unity.*

# First Read

Read "A Quilt of a Country." After you read, complete the Think Questions below.

## ☁ THINK QUESTIONS

1. Why does Quindlen refer to America as a quilt? Does this symbolism have a positive or negative connotation? Use evidence from the text to support your answer.

2. What defines "unity" in America, according to the author? Use textual evidence from paragraphs 5–7 to explain your response.

3. Quindlen mentions "pride" throughout the essay; in what ways does pride affect the cultural climate of America? Explain your answer using textual evidence.

4. The Latin word *alescere* means "to grow up." Using this knowledge and clues from the text, write your best definition of the word **coalescing**, and indicate which clues helped you with your definition.

5. Quindlen writes, "Many of the oft-told stories of the most pluralistic nation on earth are stories not of tolerance, but of **bigotry**." Using context clues from the text, write your best definition of **bigotry**.

Please note that excerpts and passages in the StudySync® library and this workbook are intended as touchstones to generate interest in an author's work. The excerpts and passages do not substitute for the reading of entire texts, and StudySync® strongly recommends that students seek out and purchase the whole literary or informational work in order to experience it as the author intended. Links to online resellers are available in our digital library. In addition, complete works may be ordered through an authorized reseller by filling out and returning to StudySync® the order form enclosed in this workbook.

Reading & Writing
Companion

**89**

# Skill:
# Figurative Language

Use the Checklist to analyze Figurative Language in "A Quilt of a Country." Refer to the sample student annotation about Figurative Language in the text.

## ••• CHECKLIST FOR FIGURATIVE LANGUAGE

In order to determine the meaning of a figure of speech in context, note the following:

✓ words that mean one thing literally and suggest something else

✓ similes, metaphors, or personification

✓ figures of speech, including

- oxymorons, or a figure of speech in which apparently contradictory terms appear in conjunction, such as

  > a description such as "deafening silence"

  > sayings such as "seriously funny"

- euphemisms, or a mild or indirect word or expression substituted for one considered to be too harsh when referring to something unpleasant or embarrassing, such as

  > saying someone has "passed away" instead of "died"

  > using the term "correctional facility" instead of "prison"

In order to interpret a figure of speech in context and analyze its role in the text, consider the following questions:

✓ Where is there figurative language in the text and what seems to be the purpose of the author's use of it?

✓ Why does the author use a figure of speech rather than literal language?

✓ How do euphemisms or oxymorons affect the meaning of the text?

✓ How does the figurative language develop the message or theme of the literary work?

# Skill:
# Figurative Language

Reread paragraph 5 of "A Quilt of a Country." Then, using the Checklist on the previous page, answer the multiple-choice questions below.

## ⟳ YOUR TURN

1. What is the BEST interpretation of Quindlen's use of the twin metaphors of "fault lines" and "electrified fences" as they are used in the first sentence?

   ○ A. The metaphors are used to describe how in the past Americans were forced to get along because of rules set down by the government.

   ○ B. The metaphors are used to describe national boundaries and protections, as a fault line in the land divides an area, or an electrified fence keeps out a common enemy.

   ○ C. The metaphor is used to describe how Americans used to be so afraid of communism that they feared their neighbors and didn't get to know each other.

   ○ D. The metaphor is used to describe the trench warfare and barbed wire that was used during World War I.

2. What is the BEST interpretation of the figure of speech, "the left side of the hyphen," as used in the second sentence?

   ○ A. The figure of speech is meant to question a person's citizenship in the country.

   ○ B. The figure of speech is describing the political "left" as opposed to the political "right."

   ○ C. The figure of speech suggests that some believe a person's ethnic identity will feel more important than his or her American identity.

   ○ D. The figure of speech is used to describe economic unrest and increasing crime.

Please note that excerpts and passages in the StudySync® library and this workbook are intended as touchstones to generate interest in an author's work. The excerpts and passages do not substitute for the reading of entire texts, and StudySync® strongly recommends that students seek out and purchase the whole literary or informational work in order to experience it as the author intended. Links to online resellers are available in our digital library. In addition, complete works may be ordered through an authorized reseller by filling out and returning to StudySync® the order form enclosed in this workbook.

Reading & Writing Companion

91

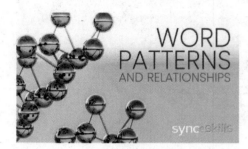

# Skill:
# Word Patterns and Relationships

Use the Checklist to analyze Word Patterns and Relationships in "A Quilt of a Country." Refer to the sample student annotations about Word Patterns and Relationships in the text.

## ••• CHECKLIST FOR WORD PATTERNS AND RELATIONSHIPS

In order to identify patterns of word changes to indicate different meanings or parts of speech, do the following:

- ✓ determine the word's part of speech

- ✓ when reading, use context clues to make a preliminary determination of the meaning of the word

- ✓ when writing a response to a text, check that you understand the meaning and part of speech and that it makes sense in your sentence

- ✓ consult a dictionary to verify your preliminary determination of the meanings and parts of speech, including morphological elements such as base or root words, prefixes, and suffixes

- ✓ be sure to read all of the definitions, and then decide which definition, form, and part of speech makes sense within the context of the text

To identify and correctly use patterns of word changes that indicate different meanings or parts of speech, consider the following questions:

- ✓ What is the intended meaning of the word?

- ✓ Do I know that this word form is the correct part of speech? Do I understand the word patterns for this particular word?

- ✓ When I consult a dictionary, can I confirm that the meaning I have determined for this word is correct? Do I know how to use it correctly?

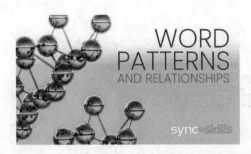

# Skill:
# Word Patterns and Relationships

Reread paragraph 4 of "A Quilt of a Country." Then, using the Checklist on the previous page, answer the multiple-choice questions below.

## YOUR TURN

1. What part of speech is the word *divisions*?

   ○ A. adjective
   ○ B. plural noun
   ○ C. verb
   ○ D. noun

2. What part of speech is the word *divided*?

   ○ A. noun
   ○ B. adjective
   ○ C. verb
   ○ D. adverb

3. What meaning is gained from analyzing the author's use of the patterns of the word changes, *divisions* and *divided*, in the context of the essay?

   ○ A. The use of the word patterns *divisions* and *divided* highlights the similarities between the United States and other countries facing similar challenging ideas.

   ○ B. The use of the word patterns *divisions* and *divided* highlights the differences between the United States and other countries facing similar challenging ideas.

   ○ C. The use of the word patterns *divisions* and then *divided* highlights the similarities and differences between the United States and other countries facing similar challenging ideas.

   ○ D. The use of the word patterns *divisions* and then *divided* highlights the ethnic differences in the United States.

# Skill:
# Arguments and Claims

Use the Checklist to analyze Arguments and Claims in "A Quilt of a Country." Refer to the sample student annotation about Arguments and Claims in the text.

## ••• CHECKLIST FOR ARGUMENTS AND CLAIMS

In order to identify the speaker's argument and claims, note the following:

✓ clues that reveal the author's opinion in the title, opening remarks, or concluding statement

✓ declarative statements that come before or follow a speaker's anecdote or story

To delineate a speaker's argument and specific claims, do the following:

✓ note the information that the speaker introduces in sequential order

✓ describe the speaker's argument in your own words

To evaluate the argument and specific claims, consider the following questions:

✓ Does the writer support each claim with reasoning and evidence?

✓ Is the reasoning sound and the evidence sufficient?

✓ Do the writer's claims work together to support the writer's overall argument?

✓ Which claims are not supported, if any?

# Skill:
# Arguments and Claims

Reread paragraph 7 of "A Quilt of a Country." Then, using the Checklist on the previous page, answer the multiple-choice questions below.

## ⟳ YOUR TURN

1. This question has two parts. First, answer Part A. Then, answer Part B.

   **Part A:** What is the author's claim in this paragraph?

   ○ A. Ma-Pa stores no longer exist in today's modern American society.

   ○ B. Modern immigrants struggle to find opportunities similar to those of earlier immigrants.

   ○ C. Calvinists are making it more difficult for immigrants to do things like ride the subway.

   ○ D. A Calvinist work ethic unifies both new immigrants and long-time Americans.

   **Part B:** What is the BEST reason or piece of evidence the author uses to support her claim?

   ○ A. "There is that Calvinist undercurrent in the American psyche"

   ○ B. "Leonel Castillo, former director of the Immigration and Naturalization Service"

   ○ C. "the new immigrants are not so different from our own parents or grandparents"

   ○ D. "Ma and Pa are now Korean, Vietnamese, Iraqi, Jordanian, Latin American."

Please note that excerpts and passages in the StudySync® library and this workbook are intended as touchstones to generate interest in an author's work. The excerpts and passages do not substitute for the reading of entire texts, and StudySync® strongly recommends that students seek out and purchase the whole literary or informational work in order to experience it as the author intended. Links to online resellers are available in our digital library. In addition, complete works may be ordered through an authorized reseller by filling out and returning to StudySync® the order form enclosed in this workbook.

Reading & Writing
Companion

95

# Close Read

Reread "A Quilt of a Country." As you reread, complete the Skills Focus questions below. Then use your answers and annotations from the questions to help you complete the Write activity.

## ◎ SKILLS FOCUS

1. Analyze Quindlen's title in relation to the essay, and explain how her use of figurative language helps her to build her argument.

2. Discuss the many times Quindlen uses some form of the word *nation*—including as singular noun, plural noun, and adjective—and explain the effect of the usage of this word on her essay. Be sure to identify and correctly use the word patterns you mention.

3. Delineate and evaluate Quindlen's central argument in this essay.

4. Analyze how the author's use of words related to the idea of difference—including *different* and *disparate*—as well as the identification of specific ethnic and religious groups help to develop and refine her ideas and claims.

5. Explain how, according to Quindlen, America's past informs its identity today.

## ✎ WRITE

EXPLANATORY: Rather than separating her essay into a series of clear claims with evidence, the author uses a string of seemingly unrelated examples to build the foundation of her argument. How does this structure help develop her central idea of America as a quilt? It might be helpful to think about how her argument or message would be changed if the essay were structured more traditionally.

# Creation Myths from Around the World

INFORMATIONAL TEXT
Angie Shumov
2016

# Introduction

A ncient cultures, without the benefit of modern science and without being in contact with one another, passed down stories to explain the natural phenomena they saw around them. Some of these stories were told to explain the oldest of mysteries, the beginning of the world itself, and they are as different as the cultures to which they were born.

# "All around the world, creation myths help us make sense of man's origin."

NOTES

1 Where did we come from and how did we get here? The answer to life's most **fundamental** question may remain unknown, but that doesn't stop narratives from telling of the world's beginning and how man came to be.

2 Neither proved right or wrong, creation myths have been passed down person to person, across generations and cultures since the beginning of time. Some speak of birth and a Supreme Being while others say the elements formed life. Even stories from the same cultural origins have different versions and **interpretations**.

## He the Creator

3 Christian, Jewish, and Islamic faiths share a common creation story. In the Book of Genesis, God says "let there be light" and in six days he creates the sun, moon, land and sky and all living creatures. He tells all to "be fruitful and multiply." Another **adaptation** goes on to speak of God creating Adam, the first man, out of the earth's dust. He then created a female companion out of Adam's rib who was given the name Eve, meaning mother of all living. Adam and Eve lived happily in God's Garden of Eden until one day, a serpent who lived in the tree of forbidden fruit, persuaded the humans to eat an apple. As God had forbidden them to touch this fruit, their disobedience brought the awareness of good and evil in the world.

## A Balanced Beginning

4 In one Chinese creation story, first there was a cosmic[1] egg made up of two balanced opposites: yin and yang. The egg held P'an Ku, the divine embryo. P'an Ku grew until the egg could not hold him, causing the shell to burst. So P'an Ku went to work right away making the world, with a hammer in hand. He dug out valleys, made way for rivers, and piled up mountains. But the earth was not complete until P'an Ku passed away. It wasn't until death that his flesh became soil and his bones the rocks. His eyes became the sun and moon

1. **cosmic** related to the universe as a whole, rather than just earth

and his head the sky. From what was once his sweat and tears was now rain and the fleas that covered his body became mankind.

## The Sacrifice

5    The earliest Vedic[2] text in the Hindu religion, the Rig Veda, tells the tale of Purusha. He who had a thousand heads, eyes, and feet could envelop the earth with his fingers. The gods sacrificed Purusha and his body turned to butter, **transforming** into animals, elements, the three gods Agni, Vayu, and Indra, and even the four castes of Hindu society. Later on, a different interpretation developed that spoke of the trinity of creation. Brahma the creator, Vishnu the preserver, and Shiva the destroyer makes a universal cycle of the world's beginning and end.

## Water of Life

6    The ancient Egyptians had numerous creation myths that all begin with the chaotic waters of Nun. Atum, while considered genderless, appeared as the first god or goddess. It is said he created himself from his thoughts and will. From the dark waters of Nun, emerged a hill for Atum to stand upon. This is where he made Shu, the god of air and Tefnut, the goddess of moisture. Shu and Tefnut created Geb, the earth, and Nut, the sky. And from Geb and Nut came even more gods and goddesses. While the world's order formed over time, Shu and Tefnut got lost in darkness. Atum sent his all-seeing eye to search for them and upon their return, he wept tears of joy. The tears struck the earth and turned into the first men.

## Three Tries

7    A Mayan creation story tells the tale of Tepeu, the maker and Gucumatz, the feathered spirit. After the two built the world with their thoughts, they decided they needed beings to look after their earth and to praise them for their creation. First, they made animals from birds and snakes to deer and panthers, but realized these creatures could not communicate their admiration. They had to produce another kind of being that was capable of worshiping them.

8    They first created man from wet clay but when he tried to speak, he crumbled apart. In a second attempt, they made men out of wood and while they could talk, they were empty headed and empty hearted, producing words with no meaning behind them. The third time around, they made four men out of the white and yellow corn. To their satisfaction, these men could think

2. **Vedic**  the language, religion, or world view of the Vedas, the Aryan precursors of the Hindu peoples and religion

and feel and speak words out of love and respect. To ensure the human race continued, the gods created women as their mates and so mankind lived on.

9. All around the world, creation myths help us make sense of man's origin. While many variations exist, these stories have built the **foundation** of the world's largest religions and cultures. There may not be a universal understanding but these legends, true or false, are the real roots of society today.

By Angie Shumov. Used by permission of National Geographic Creative.

## ✏ WRITE

PERSONAL RESPONSE: How did this text shape your understanding of the purpose of storytelling? According to this text, what meaning is attached to creation stories? Do you think humans nowadays tell stories for the same reasons or different reasons than in ancient times? Use as evidence at least one account or story of a subject told in different mediums, such as a photo on social media and a text message, in your response.

# Looking for Palestine:
## Growing Up Confused in an American-Arab Family

INFORMATIONAL TEXT

Najla Said

2013

## Introduction

Author, actress, and playwright Najla Said (b. 1974) is the daughter of leading Palestinian American intellectual Edward Said. In her memoir *Looking for Palestine: Growing Up Confused in an American-Arab Family*, she describes her life as a "hyphenated" American. In this excerpt from the beginning of the memoir, Said introduces readers to her struggle to make sense of her identity as the daughter of immigrants—and as a member of a culture about which many Americans are deeply suspicious.

# "It's mainly because of my father that people now say 'Asian American' instead of 'Oriental.'"

1   I am a Palestinian-Lebanese-American Christian woman, but I grew up as a Jew in New York City.

2   I began my life, however, as a WASP[1].

3   I was born in Boston to an Ivy League[2] literature professor and his wife, baptized into the Episcopal Church at the age of one, and, at five, sent to an all-girls private school on the Upper East Side of Manhattan, one that boasts among its alumnae such perfectly formed and well-groomed American blue bloods as the legendary Jacqueline Onassis. It was at that point that I realized that something was seriously wrong — with me.

4   With my green seersucker tunic, its matching bloomers (worn underneath for gym and dance classes), the white Peter Pan collar of my blouse, and my wool knee socks, I was every bit the Chapin[3] schoolgirl. I was proud of my new green blazer with its fancy school emblem and my elegant shoes from France. But even the most elaborate uniform could not protect against my instant awareness of my differences. I was a dark-haired rat in a sea of blond perfection. I didn't live on the Upper East Side, where everyone else in my class seemed to live, but on the Upper West Side, or, rather, so far beyond the boundaries of what was then considered the Upper West Side as to be unacceptable to many. I did not have a canopy bed, an uncluttered bedroom, and a perfectly decorated living room the way my classmates did or like the homes I saw on TV. I had books piled high on shelves and tables, pipes, pens, Oriental rugs, painted walls, and strange house guests. I was surrounded at home not only by some of the Western world's greatest scholars and writers — Noam Chomsky, Lillian Hellman, Norman Mailer, Jacques Derrida, Susan Sontag, Joan Didion — but by the creme de la creme[4] of the Palestinian Resistance[5].

---

1. **WASP** White Anglo-Saxon Protestant
2. **Ivy League** a group of eight elite, private colleges in the U.S. Northeast, including Brown, Columbia Cornell, Dartmouth, Harvard, Penn, Princeton, and Yale
3. **Chapin** a girls' school in Manhattan, New York, founded in 1901
4. **creme de la creme** (French) "the cream of the cream," i.e., the very best
5. **Palestinian Resistance** insurgency of the inhabitants of Palestine against the state of Israel after its establishment in 1948

5   I know today there are probably lots of children of immigrants growing up similarly confused by the mixed messages of their lives, pertaining to everything from class to culture to standards of beauty. For me, though, growing up the daughter of a Lebanese mother and a **prominent** Palestinian thinker in New York City in the 1980s and '90s was confusing and unsettling. I constantly questioned everything about who I was and where I fit in the world, constantly judged my own worthiness and compared myself to others, and I struggled desperately to find a way to reconcile the beautiful, comforting, loving world of my home, culture, and family with the supposed "barbaric" and "backward" place and society others perceived it to be. I wondered why I was "an exception" to the rule of what both Arabs and Americans were "supposed" to be like, and why I was stuck in such an uneasy position.

6   After years of trying desperately to convince people that they didn't really understand me or the place my family came from, I stopped trying, especially since there was never anyone around to make me feel less alone in my **assertions**. I resigned myself to believing that everything people said about my culture was true, because it was exhausting and futile to try to convince anyone otherwise. Strangely, though, I also held on tightly to what I knew to be accurate and real about my family and culture. My parents and extended family are entirely responsible for that. I spent years simultaneously pushing them away and drawing them close, until I found a place where I could exist together with them and completely apart from them. Letting go of the idea that I had to have one identity, one way to describe myself, one "real me" hasn't left me any less confused about who I am, but it has certainly left me inspired, engaged, interested, complicated, and aware. And I'd rather be all of those things than just plain old "American," or plain old "Arab."

7   With the exception of my birth in Boston and a year-and-a-half-ish stint in Palo Alto, and then Southern California, I spent the first thirteen years of my life in an apartment building on Morningside Drive between West 119th and 120th streets. My father was a "teacher of English and Comparative Lit-er-a-ture at Columbia University." I learned to pronounce that impressive-sounding title at the age of four, though I had no idea what it meant. When people asked me what my daddy's job was, I'd wrap my brain and articulators around the phrase with great effort and draw it out.

8   I did recognize the word "Columbia," and I knew what that was (the park where we played after school and on weekends). I also knew that he did something in an office in that campus-park.

9   To very smart people who study a lot, Edward Said is the "father of **postcolonial** studies" or, as he told me once when he insisted I was wasting my college education by taking a course on postmodernism and I told him he didn't even know what it was:

NOTES

10  "Know what it is, Najla? I invented it!!!" I still don't know if he was joking or serious.

11  To others, he is the author of *Orientalism*[6], the book that everyone reads at some point in college, whether in history, politics, Buddhism, or literature class. He wrote it when I was four.

12  As he explained once, when I pressed him to put it into simple English: "The basic concept, is that . . . historically, through literature and art, the 'East,' as seen through a Western lens, becomes **distorted** and degraded so that anything 'other' than what we Westerners recognize as familiar is not just exotic, mysterious, and sensual but also inherently inferior."

13  You know, like Aladdin.

14  It's mainly because of my father that people now say "Asian American" instead of "Oriental."

15  To other people, he is the symbol of Palestinian self determination, a champion of human rights, equality, and social justice. A "humanist" who "spoke truth to power."

16  And then still other people insist he was a terrorist, though anyone who knew him knows that's kind of like calling Gandhi a terrorist.

17  To me, he was my daddy, a **dapper** man in three-piece suits tailor-made in London. A cute old guy who yelled at me passionately in his weird sometimes British, sometimes American accent and then (five minutes later) forgot he had been upset; the one who brought me presents from all over the world, talked to me about Jane Eyre — my favorite book when I was twelve — and held me when I cried. He played tennis and squash, drove a Volvo, smoked a pipe, and collected pens. He was a professor. He was my father.

Excerpted from *Looking for Palestine: Growing Up Confused in an Arab-American Family* by Najla Said, published by Riverhead Books.

6. **Orientalism** a term coined by Edward W. Said in his 1978 book of the same name; it refers to the exotic aura and images projected onto Middle and Far East cultures by Western colonial nations who maintain indirect power over them

**WRITE**

ARGUMENTATIVE: The unit texts you have read so far deal with the role of traditions in shaping both individuals and communities. With these texts in mind, defend, challenge, or qualify the following statement: A person's identity is shaped by his or her surroundings. In your response, synthesize evidence from this text and at least one other text from the unit to support your position on the statement. Consider focusing on characters or speakers who react against or uphold traditions.

## Coming-of-Age Traditions from Around the World

INFORMATIONAL TEXT
Ursula Villarreal-Moura
2018

# Introduction

**studysync**

Ursula Villarreal-Moura (b. 1978) is a writer whose essays and fiction have been widely published in literary journals from *Tin House* to the *Nashville Review*. This essay surveys coming-of-age rituals from China to Mexico, from the United States to the Amazon. Read about a mitten filled with stinging ants, a dance routine that scintillated the internet, and a host of other traditions that serve as the bridge between adolescence and adulthood.

# "For those who choose to celebrate, a fun time is almost guaranteed."

NOTES

1   Entrance into adulthood is an important and oftentimes celebrated tradition around the world. Many coming-of-age traditions are considered joyous occasions marked by dancing and the lavishing of gifts while other adolescents are expected to provide evidence of their fortitude and bravery. Regardless of the rituals or requirements, becoming an adult frequently means welcoming new social expectations and duties.

2   Centuries ago, many cultures prepared younger generations for marriage, war, and other significant endeavors. Depending on the society in which young people come of age now, rites of passage can still signify a young person's maturity and their readiness to date or consider romantic relationships.

3   The timeline for when young people leave behind childhood and join the ranks of teenagers or young adults varies from culture to culture. For some, the transition is celebrated at age eleven while in other parts of the globe, a person must turn thirteen, fifteen, or, in the case of Guan Li candidates in China, men must wait until their eighteenth or twentieth birthdays.

4   In the United States, for many teenagers obtaining a driver's license or a part-time job is a **quintessential** rite of passage. Whereas previously the teen was dependent on a parent, guardian, or friend for transportation needs, with the ability to drive comes newfound freedom—even if it requires sharing a vehicle. Similarly, an after-school or summer job is often a teen's first taste of financial independence, one hallmark of adulthood.

5   While many young people enjoy partaking in long-standing cultural traditions, not everyone finds these rites of passage representative of their emerging identity. For some individuals, status quo traditions serve as a reminder of times when social or cultural obligations were rarely questioned, and people behaved as was expected of them. Such rituals may be rooted in religious beliefs or strict standards regarding gender roles. Some customs have evolved with time to suit current generations, who might wish for less public pomp and circumstance.

 Skill: Textual Evidence

*Gaining freedom and financial independence is "one hallmark of adulthood," supported by explicit evidence: getting a driver's license and a part-time job are rites of passage, like an American declaration of independence.*

6   For those who choose to celebrate, a fun time is almost guaranteed. After all, nothing confirms some *joie de vivre* like a boisterous party.

**Quinceañera**

7   The Latin American counterpart to the Sweet Sixteen celebration is the *quinceañera*. Quinceañeras, believed to have originated in Mexico, mark the end of a young girl's childhood and her introduction into society as a mature young woman. Celebrated when girls are fifteen, quinceañeras are lavish **soirees** in which the honoree dons an extravagant ball gown. Accessories often include expensive jewelry and a tiara.

8   Celebration festivities traditionally begin with a Catholic mass in which the young girl renews her baptismal commitment and is blessed by a priest, godparents, and her parents. Part of her shift from childhood into womanhood is marked by vows to honor herself, her family, and her religion.

9   Festivities typically include several rounds of dancing and meals, a candle ceremony, and a toast made to the quinceañera herself. Often the price of such a celebration can range up to several thousands of dollars, with high-ticket items including the honoree's dress and jewelry, hired photographers, live music, catered food, and an enormous cake, as well as gifts the young woman can use as she transitions into womanhood.

A photograph of a young woman on her quinceanera day.

10    In 2016, a Houston native named Jasmine Cortinas decided she wanted her quinceañera to be memorable for guests as well as representative of her musical tastes. While a father-daughter dance is traditionally part of the party's events, Jasmine opted for a dance routine that incorporated contemporary music and dance styles that would challenge both her and her father's dance skills. The result was a choreographed dance routine that went viral on YouTube and likely inspired many other young women to tailor their own celebrations to their unique tastes and personalities.

11    While most quinceañeras are well attended, in 2016 Rubi Ibarra's party invitation went viral on Facebook after her father publicly posted details about his daughter's celebration, allowing the time and location of the bash to be shared by thousands of users. While the party in the northern Mexico town of Villa de Guadalupe was intended solely for Rubi's friends and family, over a million people from all over the world RSVPed. In total, between 20,000 and 30,000 people were reported to have attended her birthday. In addition to the party's lineup of many rounds of catered food, and plenty of dancing and live music, it included an outdoor horse race.

## Tchoodi

12    In the West Africa country of Mali, Fulani women undergo a facial tattooing process known interchangeably as *tchoodi* or *socou-gol*. In order to avoid mockery by peers and signal their readiness to marry, beginning at puberty young girls signal their bravery by allowing other women to darken their lips, mouth, and oftentimes gums with black ink. The ritual occurs while the fully conscious young girl lays on her back as older Fulani women transform her face from girlhood to womanhood.

13    During the custom, black pigment is applied by repeatedly poking an ink-soaked scorching needle or sharp piece of wood into the young girl's lips and the surrounding facial area. A time-consuming process, tchoodi causes profuse bleeding and swelling, which Fulani girls are expected to endure with stoicism and bravery. Such coloring is believed to highlight a girl's smile and her white teeth, a sign of exquisite beauty and fertility in the culture.

14    Since dark lips and a ringed mouth are considered aesthetically attractive, Fulani men are expected to marry young women who have undergone this beautification ritual. Women aren't the only ones believed to become more attractive with pigmentation, though. In neighboring Senegal, Fulani men often undergo a similar process in which their gums are blackened. This related custom is considered both a marker of attraction as well as a sign of dental health in their community.

**Skill: Textual Evidence**

*I can infer that personalizing a coming-of-age tradition is rewarding. The author states that because Jasmine personalized her dance routine to her tastes, she likely inspired other girls to do the same.*

NOTES

Copyright © BookheadEd Learning, LLC

NOTES

This teenage girl's facial tattoo is evidence of her entrance into womanhood.

15 **Recovery** time for tchoodi can last up to three weeks, when young girls subsist on liquids ingested through a straw. Since bravery is an integral part of this African culture, girls are not known to shy away from the ritual. In fact, continuing the Fulani way of life and custom—known as *pulaaku*— is of utmost importance to the tribe and enduring tchoodi is one way in which traditions live on generation after generation.

### Sateré-Mawé

16 In the Amazon, young Sateré-Mawé boys prove their readiness to become warriors by enduring an agonizing **initiation** known as *dança da tucandeira*, involving many tucandeiras or poisonous bullet ants.

17 At age 13, Sateré-Mawé boys enter the jungle to hunt for bullet ants to use for their initiation ritual. Hundreds of bullet ants are first sedated then woven onto palm frond gloves resembling oven mitts. Ants stingers are intentionally woven pointing inward as the goal is to endure as much pain as nature intends. In preparation for the endurance test, youths have their hands and forearms covered in a black paint that is said to protect them from the inevitable stings.

18 Sateré-Mawé boys are fitted with the mitts and subjected to the ants stinging for up to ten minutes at a time. Considered thirty times more painful than a bee sting, the pain of a bullet ant bite is sometimes likened to being shot, hence the name "bullet" ant. Ant venom causes the boys' hands and arms to

swell and it is common for the initiant to experience temporary paralysis or convulsions following the ritual. Few boys are said to cry out, as manhood among the Sateré-Mawé is defined by tolerance to agony. However, the relief of removing the mitt is short-lived as the process will be repeated up to twenty times over several months in order for the boy to prove his manhood.

**Ji Li and Guan Li**

19 An ancient tradition, the Confucian coming-of-age ceremonies of *Ji Li* (笄禮 or hair pinning) and *Guan Li* (冠禮 or capping) are now experiencing a resurgence. Known as coronation ceremonies, the rituals involve both young women and young men having their hair pinned or capped as proof of their sexual maturity and readiness to marry.

20 In China, the coming-of-age tradition Ji Li occurs for young women at age fifteen, and for young men between the ages of eighteen and twenty. The ceremony involves wearing traditional Han clothing and includes honoring Huangdi, a former emperor.

21 Since having long, strong hair is considered a symbol of beauty, some young girls in China wear their hair in braids until their Ji Li ceremony. The initiation involves honorees having their hair washed, parted, and pulled into a knot or bun. The gathered hair is then held tight with pins made of wood, jade, or gold. Modern-day Ji Li celebrations are community affairs with groups of girls publicly taking vows of adulthood.

A Ji Li honoree is attended to by an elder who prepares her hair.

Reading & Writing Companion

22 Prior to Guan Li, a young man is required to select a guest of honor to perform the ceremony, typically a teacher, and another guest to cap him. During the ritual, the honoree is presented with a cap and scarf. In the presence of his family, his hair is pulled into a bun and he is capped by his chosen assistant after which the young man delivers a speech. Given the importance of respect, the honoree bows and kneels throughout the ceremony to his teacher and parents, and listens as they offer advice and usher him into the next stage of his **development**.

23 Part of the coronation ceremony for Ji Li and Guan Li includes honorees receiving a courtesy or style name that replaces their birth name and welcomes them as adults with new responsibilities. Style names may be self-selected by the honoree or chosen by a mentor, teacher, or parent.

**Celebrating the Transition From Child to Adult**

24 Youths across the globe embrace passage into adulthood in a variety of styles and manners. All the traditions discussed—quinceañera, tchoodi, dança da tucandeira, and Ji Li and Guan Li—involve participation from parents, mentors, or community members.

25 Often, traditions can be modernized to reflect contemporary styles or attitudes as evidenced by Jasmine Cortinas' choreographed father-daughter dance. Other times preserving traditions for decades is a sign of respect and unwavering dedication to one's ancestors, as in the case of tchoodi.

26 Sometimes the journey from childhood to adulthood happens without much fanfare. Gaining the right to vote and to enlist in the military are two long-standing American rites of passage that occur when a teen turns eighteen. Exercising the right to vote imbues an individual with a political voice and the potential to shape far-reaching legislative policies. Likewise, joining the the military is an opportunity to demonstrate patriotism through service to our country. Both these coming of age traditions acknowledge increased expectations that accompany mature citizenship.

27 All rites of passage, whether private or public, near or far, serve as important milestones for generation after generation.

# First Read

Read "Coming-of-Age Traditions from Around the World." After you read, complete the Think Questions below.

## ☁ THINK QUESTIONS

1. How are driver's licenses and after-school jobs steps toward adulthood in America? Explain, citing evidence from the text.

2. How do quinceañeras and the Chinese coming-of-age traditions involve elders of the community? Cite evidence from the text to support your answer.

3. Explain what rituals from the text have evolved to include more "modern tastes" and which rituals have adhered to tradition. Refer to the text as you develop your answer.

4. Use context clues to determine the meaning of **soiree** as it is used in the text. Write your best definition, along with a brief explanation of the which clues helped you determine its meaning.

5. Keeping in mind that the Latin word *initiō* means "to begin," what do you think the word **initiation** means as it is used in the text? Write your definition, and explain how you determined its meaning.

Please note that excerpts and passages in the StudySync® library and this workbook are intended as touchstones to generate interest in an author's work. The excerpts and passages do not substitute for the reading of entire texts, and StudySync® strongly recommends that students seek out and purchase the whole literary or informational work in order to experience it as the author intended. Links to online resellers are available in our digital library. In addition, complete works may be ordered through an authorized reseller by filling out and returning to StudySync® the order form enclosed in this workbook.

Reading & Writing Companion 113

# Skill:
# Textual Evidence

Use the Checklist to analyze Textual Evidence in "Coming-of-Age Traditions from Around the World." Refer to the sample student annotations about Textual Evidence in the text.

## ••• CHECKLIST FOR TEXTUAL EVIDENCE

In order to support an analysis by citing evidence that is explicitly stated in the text, do the following:

✓ Read the text closely and critically.

✓ Identify what the text says explicitly.

✓ Find the most relevant textual evidence that supports your analysis.

✓ Consider why an author explicitly states specific details.

✓ Cite the specific words, phrases, lines, or stanzas from the text that support your analysis.

In order to interpret implicit meanings in a text by making inferences, do the following:

✓ Combine information directly stated in the text with your own knowledge, experiences, and observations.

✓ Cite the specific words, phrases, sentences, or paragraphs from the text that led to and support this inference.

In order to cite textual evidence to support an analysis of what the text says explicitly as well as inferences drawn from the text, consider the following questions:

✓ Have I read the text closely and critically?

✓ What inferences am I making about the text?

✓ What textual evidence am I using to support these inferences?

✓ Am I quoting the evidence from the text correctly?

✓ Does my textual evidence logically relate to my analysis or the inference I am making?

# Skill:
# Textual Evidence

Reread paragraph 15 of "Coming-of-Age Traditions from Around the World." Then, using the Checklist on the previous page, answer the multiple-choice questions below.

## ⟳ YOUR TURN

1. This question has two parts. First, answer Part A. Then, answer Part B.

   **Part A:** What can be inferred about important coming-of-age traditions in this paragraph?

   ○ A. Preserving a cultural tradition is more important than temporary discomfort.

   ○ B. Women have more pain tolerance than men during rituals in the Fulani culture.

   ○ C. Coming-of-age traditions like this one should be modernized.

   ○ D. Traditions that have an element of pain endurance should be more respected than others.

   **Part B:** Which piece of textual evidence BEST supports your answer from Part A?

   ○ A. "Since bravery is an integral part of this African culture, girls are not known to shy away from the ritual."

   ○ B. "In fact, continuing the Fulani way of life and custom—known as *pulaaku*— is of utmost importance to the tribe"

   ○ C. "enduring tchoodi is one way in which traditions live on generation after generation"

   ○ D. "Recovery time for tchoodi can last up to three weeks."

COMING-OF-AGE
TRADITIONS
FROM AROUND THE WORLD

# Close Read

Reread "Coming-of-Age Traditions from Around the World." As you reread, complete the Skills Focus questions below. Then use your answers and annotations from the questions to help you complete the Write activity.

## ◎ SKILLS FOCUS

1. Highlight details in the text that suggest complex emotions are involved in coming-of-age traditions. Cite strong textual evidence to explain several emotions that are evoked.

2. Identify the author's purpose in writing this essay and explain how the author's choice of language helps to support that purpose.

3. Discuss how the use of headings, photographs, and captions helps to connect sections of text.

4. Analyze how rites of passage, according to this essay, affect the lives of the people who celebrate them.

## ✏ WRITE

DISCUSSION: Traditions are customs, stories, beliefs, rituals, and/or routines that are passed down in a family from one generation to another. Research has proven that traditions are part of healthy families, provide a foundation for shared identity, and help build strong bonds between generations. In your opinion, what positive effects can traditions have on individuals, families, and/or communities? Synthesize textual evidence from this text and at least one other text from the unit, as well as relevant personal anecdotes, to support your answer to this question. To prepare for the discussion, write down your thoughts about this question and explain your reasoning.

Extended Writing Project and Grammar

EXTENDED WRITING PROJECT
RESEARCH WRITING

# Research Writing Process: Plan

| PLAN | DRAFT | REVISE | EDIT AND PUBLISH |
| --- | --- | --- | --- |

Mythologist Joseph Campbell once said, "If you're going to have a story, have a big story, or none at all." People across time and place have invented ways to explain how we came to be the way we are now. Origin stories can play a role in nations, families, cultures, and religions. Examples of origin stories include the biblical story of Genesis, the Iroquois story of the Great Turtle, and the Greek story of Zeus.

## WRITING PROMPT

**What do origin stories reveal about our perceptions of the world?**

Choose one origin story relating to a religion, culture, or nation that you would like to learn more about. Write a research paper explaining this origin story and how it has shaped a particular community. As part of your research process, select a research question, develop a research plan, gather and evaluate source materials, and synthesize and present your research findings. Regardless of which origin story you choose, be sure your research project includes the following:

- an introduction
- relevant information synthesized from at least three authoritative print and digital sources
- a clear text structure
- appropriate formatting, graphics, and multimedia, as needed
- a conclusion
- citations for sources

### Writing to Sources

As you gather ideas and information from a variety of authoritative print and digital sources, be sure to:

- use and cite evidence from multiple sources;
- avoid plagiarism, or including source information without credit; and
- avoid overly relying on one source.

## Introduction to Informative Research Writing

Informative research writing examines a topic and conveys ideas and information through comparisons, description, and explanation. Good informative research writing includes genre characteristics and craft, such as a clear **thesis statement** and **supporting facts and details** from **reliable sources** that clarify and support the central idea or thesis statement. The characteristics of informative research writing include:

- an **introduction** with a clear controlling idea or thesis statement
- **body paragraphs** with supporting details, such as definitions, quotations, examples, and facts that are cited accurately and back up the central idea or thesis
- a clear and logical **text structure**
- a **formal style**
- integration of **print features**, such as headers; **graphics**, such as maps or charts; and **multimedia**, including audio or video, as needed for comprehension
- a **conclusion** that wraps up your ideas
- proper citation of sources, including a **works cited list**

In addition to these characteristics, writers also carefully narrow the focus of their research by generating research questions and developing a research plan. The research process requires patience as you evaluate the validity and usefulness of sources related to your topic. Researchers develop over time their skills of locating and assessing the appropriateness of a source.

As you continue with this Extended Writing Project, you'll receive more instruction and practice at crafting each of the characteristics of informative research writing to create your own Informative research paper.

Please note that excerpts and passages in the StudySync® library and this workbook are intended as touchstones to generate interest in an author's work. The excerpts and passages do not substitute for the reading of entire texts, and StudySync® strongly recommends that students seek out and purchase the whole literary or informational work in order to experience it as the author intended. Links to online resellers are available in our digital library. In addition, complete works may be ordered through an authorized reseller by filling out and returning to StudySync® the order form enclosed in this workbook.

Reading & Writing Companion    **119**

Before you get started on your own informative research paper, read this paper that one student, Josh, wrote in response to the writing prompt. As you read the Model, highlight and annotate the features of informative research writing that Josh included in his paper.

## ☰ STUDENT MODEL

### The *Popol* Vuh and the Maya: Keeping Meaning Across Time

#### The Maya Beginning

1 "Who am I?" and "How do I fit into this world?" are not just questions we ask ourselves as we grow up. These questions have been around for ages. To answer these important life questions, ancient humans used observations and imagination to explain how things came to be. The world's oldest cultures developed origin stories that explain the existence of good and evil, for example, as well as the creation of earth, sky, water, crops, animals, and humans. The Maya of what is now Guatemala are one such ancient culture. Part of their origin story, the *Popol Vuh*, describes how the gods created humankind after multiple failed attempts. Carefully studying the *Popol Vuh* and the research around it provides insight into how the Maya have understood time, the divine, and human nature. Studying ancient texts like the *Popol Vuh* serves to remind all human beings of the distances human progress has traveled through centuries, and also how much wisdom the ancients had that is still worth understanding today.

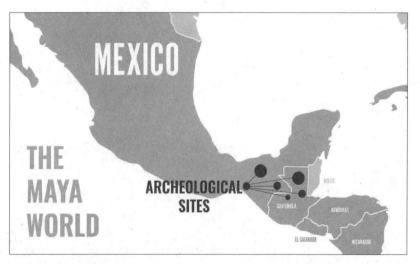

Spreading from what is now Guatemala and beyond, the Maya civilization was one of the most advanced in what is now Latin America. ("The Maya World")

### A Book for the Ages

2 According to Lewis Spence, translator of a 1908 English edition of the *Popol Vuh*, "The name 'Popol Vuh' signifies 'Record of the Community,' and its literal translation is 'Book of the Mat,' from the Kiché word 'pop' or 'popol,' a mat or rug of woven rushes or bark on which the entire family sat, and 'vuh' or 'uuh,' paper or book, from 'uoch' to write" (Spence). For centuries, the *Popol Vuh* has shaped Maya understanding of life as a cycle. The story begins with the gods gathering to create the earth. After building the world, the gods wanted to fill it with creatures who would worship them (Shumov).

3 • First, they created humans from wet clay, but these humans could not speak, so the gods destroyed them in a flood.

4 • On their second attempt, the gods created humans out of wood; however, as Shumov explains, while these humans could talk, "they were empty headed and empty hearted." So, the gods destroyed the human race a second time.

5 • Finally, on the third attempt, the gods "made four men out of the white and yellow corn" and were satisfied that "these men could think and feel and speak words out of love and respect" (Shumov). In Maria Gomez's retelling, these humans were actually "too wise." Rather than destroy the human race for a third time, however, one of the gods "clouded their minds and eyes so they would become less wise" (Gomez).

6 This ancient story told in the *Popol Vuh* shows the power of the gods and reveals a cycle of creation and destruction that has shaped the way the Maya understand time, the divine, and their rulers.

### Humanity in Time

7 The three creations of humanity, as described in the *Popol Vuh*, have had a great influence on Maya culture, which can be seen in the Maya's relationship with time. Because gods destroyed humanity twice before, the Maya believe the gods could do so again. However, because humans were then re-created, the Maya believe this, too, will happen again. These interpretations of the *Popol Vuh* relate to the Maya belief in time as an endless cycle of beginnings and endings. To record these never-ending cycles of creation and

Please note that excerpts and passages in the StudySync® library and this workbook are intended as touchstones to generate interest in an author's work. The excerpts and passages do not substitute for the reading of entire texts, and StudySync® strongly recommends that students seek out and purchase the whole literary or informational work in order to experience it as the author intended. Links to online resellers are available in our digital library. In addition, complete works may be ordered through an authorized reseller by filling out and returning to StudySync® the order form enclosed in this workbook.

Reading & Writing Companion

121

NOTES

destruction, the Maya invented "one of the most accurate calendar systems in human history" ("The Calendar System"). The Calendar Round records dates 52 days into the future (Mark). The Long Count Calendar, started in 3114 BCE, calculates dates far into the future. The current cycle started in December 2012. This way of timekeeping is still seen in Maya society today. To track the different cycles of time, Maya communities have "daykeepers." Daykeepers are responsible for keeping the cycles going with the proper rituals and ceremonies. Drawing on centuries of knowledge, they keep track of the calendar, and serve as healers for the Maya people ("The Modern Calendar Priests"). In Maya culture, a calendar is more than a grid or list of dates used for keeping appointments; this calendar encompasses entire life cycles.

This shows the features of a Calendar Round. One view of the daykeepers is that the world is constantly dying, and the daykeepers reset it. ("The Modern Calendar Priests," Getty Images)

8    Beyond the Calendar Round, the Maya origin story has also influenced the Maya's understanding of divine forces and human nature. According to the *Popol Vuh*, humanity was created in order to worship the gods. The gods are to be respected because they have the power to both create and destroy humanity. This aspect of their religion can be seen in the Maya pyramids. The structure of the pyramids is symbolic. For example, the pyramids were built with flat tops, which created space on which rituals of bloodletting and human sacrifice could be performed to honor the gods by returning "life force" to them (Jarus). In addition to emphasizing Maya respect for

the gods, ancient Maya structures also reveal Maya understanding of human nature. In the city of Palenque, an ancient burial tomb for a Maya king, Pakal, was discovered in 1952. This tomb is decorated with carvings that show the king's ancestors as well as his rebirth (Jarus). These depictions of the king's life, death, and rebirth reveal a belief in life as a series of beginnings and endings and connect back to the cycle of creation and destruction described in the *Popol Vuh*.

**The Web of Life**

9 Thousands of years ago, the Maya first told creation stories in an attempt to understand the world and to answer life's big questions, such as "Who am I?," "Why am I here?," and "Why is the world the way it is?" In attempting to answer these questions, the Maya origin stories described the world and beyond as places "where time is cyclical and all things are interconnected" ("Connecting Earth and Sky"). In other words, time is an intricately woven web that connects all beings and events. These creation stories also describe a special bond between humanity and the gods, as well as a careful balance of creation and destruction. Indeed, for the Maya who are alive today, these stories serve as an important cultural foundation and link to the past. For the world, links to ancient cultures can serve as guideposts: no matter what the future holds, human beings must find a way, as the Daykeepers did, to adjust their settings and keep on going.

Please note that excerpts and passages in the StudySync® library and this workbook are intended as touchstones to generate interest in an author's work. The excerpts and passages do not substitute for the reading of entire texts, and StudySync® strongly recommends that students seek out and purchase the whole literary or informational work in order to experience it as the author intended. Links to online resellers are available in our digital library. In addition, complete works may be ordered through an authorized reseller by filling out and returning to StudySync® the order form enclosed in this workbook.

Reading & Writing Companion    **123**

NOTES

## Works Cited

"The Calendar System." *Living Maya Time: Sun, Corn, and the Calendar*, Smithsonian National Museum of the American Indian, maya.nmai. si.edu/calendar/calendar-system. Accessed 8 Apr. 2018.

"Connecting Earth and Sky." *Living Maya Time: Sun, Corn, and the Calendar*, Smithsonian National Museum of the American Indian, maya.nmai.si.edu/the-maya/connecting-earth-and-sky. Accessed 7 Apr. 2018.

Gomez, Maria C. "Maya Religion." *Ancient History Encyclopedia*, www.ancient.eu/Maya_Religion/#references. Accessed 8 Apr. 2018.

Jarus, Owen. "The Maya: History, Culture & Religion." *LiveScience*, 22 Aug. 2017, www.livescience.com/41781-the-maya.html. Accessed 9 Apr. 2018.

Mark, Joshua J. "Maya Civilization." *Ancient History Encyclopedia*, www.ancient.eu/Maya_Civilization/. Accessed 8 Apr. 2018.

"The Maya World." *Living Maya Time: Sun, Corn, and the Calendar*, Smithsonian National Museum of the American Indian, maya.nmai.si.edu/the-maya/maya-world. Accessed 7 Apr. 2018.

"The Modern Calendar Priests." *Archaeology Magazine*, www.archaeology.org/issues/44-1211/features/306-calendar-priests. Accessed 8 Apr. 2018.

Shumov, Angie. "Creation Myths from Around the World." StudySync. 2016.

Spence, Lewis. "The Popol Vuh." *Project Gutenberg.* 1908. http://www.gutenberg.org/files/56550/56550-h/56550-h.htm. Accessed 4 Apr. 2018.

## ✏ WRITE

When writing, first consider your purpose, keeping in mind who your audience is so you can write appropriately for them. Your audience for this project consists of your teacher and peers, and your purpose is implied within the writing prompt. Reread the prompt to determine your purpose for writing.

To begin, review the questions below and then select a strategy, such as brainstorming, journaling, reading, or discussing, to generate ideas.

After generating ideas, begin the prewriting process by writing a summary of your writing plan. In your summary, respond to the following questions:

- **Purpose:** Which origin story would you like to write about? What does it tell us about the culture it came from?

- **Audience:** Who is your audience? What background information will you need to include about your topic? What new information do you want them to learn?

- **Question:** How can you use a research question to focus your research?

- **Sources:** What kinds of sources will help you answer that question?

- **Structure:** How can you effectively share the information you find with readers?

### Response Instructions

Use the questions in the bulleted list to write a one-paragraph summary. Your summary should describe what you plan to research and inform your audience about in this research paper. Include possible research questions of your own based on the prompt.

Don't worry about including all of the details now; focus only on the most essential and important elements. You will refer back to this short summary as you continue through the steps of the writing process.

Please note that excerpts and passages in the StudySync® library and this workbook are intended as touchstones to generate interest in an author's work. The excerpts and passages do not substitute for the reading of entire texts, and StudySync® strongly recommends that students seek out and purchase the whole literary or informational work in order to experience it as the author intended. Links to online resellers are available in our digital library. In addition, complete works may be ordered through an authorized reseller by filling out and returning to StudySync® the order form enclosed in this workbook.

Reading & Writing Companion    125

# Skill:
# Planning Research

In order to conduct a short or more sustained research project to answer a question or solve a problem, do the following:

- Select a topic or problem to research.

- Think about what you want to find out and where you might search.

- Start to formulate your major research question by asking open-ended questions that begin "How...?" and "Why...?" and choose one that you are interested in exploring.

- Narrow or broaden your inquiry when appropriate, sorting information or items so they are easily distinguishable from one another.

- Locate multiple sources on the subject to:

  > synthesize information from different points of view.

  > demonstrate understanding of the subject under investigation.

In order to conduct a short or more sustained research project to answer a question or solve a problem, consider the following questions:

- Does the question allow me to explore a new issue, an important problem worth solving, or a fresh perspective on a topic?

- Can I research my question within my given time frame and with the resources available to me?

- Can I synthesize information from multiple sources on the question or problem, looking for different points of view?

- Will I be able to demonstrate understanding of the subject under investigation in my research project?

YOUR TURN

Read the research questions below. Then, complete the chart by matching each question into the correct category.

| Research Questions | |
|---|---|
| A | What does the Chinese creation story tell us about the prominence of nature in ancient Chinese culture? |
| B | How many different origin stories exist in China and how have they changed over time? |
| C | What are some Egyptian creation stories? |
| D | What was the relationship of ancient Egyptians to bodies of water? |
| E | What artistic representation best reveals how the Chinese creation story portrays nature? |
| F | What do Egyptian stories tell us about the ancient Egyptians' relationship with nature? |

| Too Narrow | Appropriate | Too Broad |
|---|---|---|
| | | |
| | | |
| | | |

Please note that excerpts and passages in the StudySync® library and this workbook are intended as touchstones to generate interest in an author's work. The excerpts and passages do not substitute for the reading of entire texts, and StudySync® strongly recommends that students seek out and purchase the whole literary or informational work in order to experience it as the author intended. Links to online resellers are available in our digital library. In addition, complete works may be ordered through an authorized reseller by filling out and returning to StudySync® the order form enclosed in this workbook.

Reading & Writing Companion    127

**YOUR TURN**

With your teacher's guidance, generate questions for formal research. Using the questions in the checklist, evaluate each question to determine whether it is too narrow, too broad, or just right. Select a just-right question. Then, complete the chart by writing a short plan for how you will go about doing research for your paper.

| Questions | My Response |
|---|---|
| Possible Research Questions: | |
| Selected Research Question: | |
| Step 1: | |
| Step 2: | |
| Step 3: | |

# Skill:
# Evaluating Sources

## ••• CHECKLIST FOR EVALUATING SOURCES

First, reread the sources you gathered and identify the following:

- what kind of source it is, including video, audio, or text, and where the source comes from
- where information seems inaccurate, biased, or outdated
- where information seems irrelevant or tangential to your research question

In order to use advanced searches to gather relevant, credible, and accurate print and digital sources, use the following questions as a guide:

- Is the material published by a well-established source or expert author?
- Is the material up-to-date or based on the most current information?
- Is the material factual, and can it be verified by another source?
- Are there specific terms or phrases in my research question that I can use to adjust my search?
- Can I use "and," "or," or "not" to expand or limit my search?
- Can I use quotation marks to search for exact phrases?

In order to integrate multiple sources of information presented in diverse media formats, ask the following:

- Have I included information from a variety of media?

- Am I relying too heavily on one source or source type?

- Have I varied the points at which I reference a particular source over the course of the speech or paper?

- As I listen to a presentation, am I aware of the speaker's use of sources? Where applicable, do the diverse media formats work well together?

YOUR TURN

Read the factors below. Then, complete the chart by sorting them into those that show a source is credible and reliable and those that do not.

| Factors | |
|---|---|
| A | The website is a personal blog written by a person who enjoys learning about the subject matter. |
| B | The author is a journalist working for an internationally recognized newspaper. |
| C | The text avoids personal judgments and includes several different viewpoints that are properly cited. |
| D | The article states only the author's personal opinions and leaves out other positions as well as sources. |
| E | The text relies on questionable premises and broad generalizations to persuade readers. |
| F | The article includes citations and a list of sources the author referenced. |

| Credible and Reliable | Not Credible or Reliable |
|---|---|
| | |
| | |
| | |

## ⟳ YOUR TURN

Complete the chart below by filling in the title and author of a source and answering questions about it.

| Source Title and Author: _____ | |
| --- | --- |
| **Reliability:** Has the source material been published in a well-established book, periodical, or website? | |
| **Reliability:** Is the source material up-to-date or based on the most current information? | |
| **Credibility:** Is the source material written by a recognized expert on the topic? | |
| **Credibility:** Is the source material published by a well-respected author or organization? | |
| **Bias:** Is the source material connected to persons or organizations that are objective and unbiased? | |
| **Evaluation:** Is this a source I should use in my project? | |

Please note that excerpts and passages in the StudySync® library and this workbook are intended as touchstones to generate interest in an author's work. The excerpts and passages do not substitute for the reading of entire texts, and StudySync® strongly recommends that students seek out and purchase the whole literary or informational work in order to experience it as the author intended. Links to online resellers are available in our digital library. In addition, complete works may be ordered through an authorized reseller by filling out and returning to StudySync® the order form enclosed in this workbook.

Reading & Writing Companion    **131**

# Skill:
# Research and Notetaking

In order to conduct short as well as more sustained research projects to answer a question (including a self-generated question) or solve a problem, do the following:

- answer a question for a research project, or think of your own, self-generated question that you would like to have answered

- look up your topic in an encyclopedia to find general information

- find specific, up-to-date information in books and periodicals, on the Internet, and if appropriate, from interviews with experts

- narrow or broaden your inquiry when appropriate

  > if you find dozens of books on a topic, your research topic may be too broad

  > if it is difficult to write a research question, narrow your topic so it is more specific

- synthesize your information by organizing your notes from various sources to see what they have in common and how they differ

To conduct short as well as more sustained research projects to answer a question (including a self-generated question) or solve a problem, consider the following questions:

- Where could I look to find additional information?

- How does new information I have found affect my research question?

- How can I demonstrate understanding of the subject I am investigating?

## ↻ YOUR TURN

Read the notes from a student's research below. Then, complete the chart by sorting them into those that are relevant and those that are not relevant to the topic of what the Chinese origin story of Pan Gu reveals about the Chinese people's attitude toward divine forces.

| Notes | |
|---|---|
| A | According to one Chinese origin story, the first man was named Pan Gu. He separated heaven and earth and divided the seas. |
| B | The Mien people of southern China primarily believe in Daoism, which is focused on the origin story of Pan Gu. |
| C | One important principle that surfaces throughout the story of Pan Gu is the idea of "inescapable duality." |
| D | Representations of Pan Gu are embroidered on many traditional Chinese items of clothing. |

| Relevant to Topic | Not Relevant to Topic |
|---|---|
| | |
| | |

Please note that excerpts and passages in the StudySync® library and this workbook are intended as touchstones to generate interest in an author's work. The excerpts and passages do not substitute for the reading of entire texts, and StudySync® strongly recommends that students seek out and purchase the whole literary or informational work in order to experience it as the author intended. Links to online resellers are available in our digital library. In addition, complete works may be ordered through an authorized reseller by filling out and returning to StudySync® the order form enclosed in this workbook.

Reading & Writing Companion

133

**YOUR TURN**

Complete the chart by synthesizing and recording information from each of four sources relevant to your subject. Remember to number and cite each source.

| Information from Sources | Synthesis |
|---|---|
|  |  |
|  |  |
|  |  |
|  |  |

# Research Writing Process: Draft

| PLAN | DRAFT | REVISE | EDIT AND PUBLISH |
|------|-------|--------|------------------|

You have already made progress toward writing your research paper. Now it is time to draft your research paper.

## ✏ WRITE

Use your plan and other responses in your Binder to draft your research paper. You may also have new ideas as you begin drafting. Feel free to explore those new ideas as you have them. You can also ask yourself these questions to ensure that your writing is focused, organized, and developed:

**Draft Checklist:**

☐ **Focused:** Have I made my thesis statement clear to readers? Have I included only relevant information and details and nothing extraneous that might confuse my readers?

☐ **Organized:** Does the organizational structure in my paper make sense? Will readers be engaged by the organization and interested in the way I present information and evidence?

☐ **Developed:** Does my writing flow together naturally, or is it choppy? Will my readers be able to follow my ideas? Will they understand the purpose of my research?

Before you submit your draft, read it over carefully. You want to be sure that you've responded to all aspects of the prompt.

Please note that excerpts and passages in the StudySync® library and this workbook are intended as touchstones to generate interest in an author's work. The excerpts and passages do not substitute for the reading of entire texts, and StudySync® strongly recommends that students seek out and purchase the whole literary or informational work in order to experience it as the author intended. Links to online resellers are available in our digital library. In addition, complete works may be ordered through an authorized reseller by filling out and returning to StudySync® the order form enclosed in this workbook.

Reading & Writing Companion   **135**

Here is Josh's informative research paper draft. As you read, notice how Josh develops his draft to be focused, organized, and developed. As he continues to revise and edit his paper, he will find and improve weak spots in his writing, as well as correct any language or punctuation mistakes.

NOTES

Skill: Print and Graphic Features

Josh adds headings throughout his paper to group the information and help readers better understand his thesis. By including print and graphic features, as well as synthesizing multiple sources, including multimedia sources, Josh communicates information more effectively and supports his thesis in a more thorough manner.

## ☰ STUDENT MODEL: FIRST DRAFT

### The *Popol Vuh* and the Maya

### The Maya Beginning

To answer important life questions, ancient humans came up with creation stories. The world's oldest cultures all have origin stories that explain good and evil and telling the creation of earth, sky, water, crops, animals, and humans. The Maya were one such ancient culture. Part of their origin story, the *Popol Vuh*, describes how the gods created humankind after multiple, failed attempts. Carefully studying the *Popol Vuh* provides insight into how the Maya have understood time, the divine and human nature.

### A Book for the Ages

The Popol Vuh has shaped Mayan understanding of life as a cycel. The story begins with the gods gathering to create the earth. After building the world, the gods wanted to fill it with creatures who would worship them. First they created humans from wet clay, but these humans could not speak so the gods destroyed them in a flood. On their second attempt the gods created men out of wood, however, while these men could talk, they were empty headed and empty hearted. So the gods destroyed the human race a second time. ~~Finaly on the third attempt the gods made four men out of white and yellow corn and satisfied that these men could think and feel and speak words out of love and respect. In one retelling, these humans were actualy "too wise." Rather than destroy the human race for a third time, however, one of the gods "clouded their minds and eyes so they would become less wise." This ancient story told in the Popol Vuh shows the power of the gods and reveals a cycel of creation and destruction that has shaped the way the Maya understand time, the divine, and their rulers.~~

- Finally, on the third attempt, the gods "made four men out of the white and yellow corn" and were satisfied that "these men could think and feel and speak words out of love and respect" (Shumov). In Maria Gomez's retelling, these humans were actually "too wise." Rather than destroy the human race for a third time, however, one of the gods "clouded their minds and eyes so they would become less wise" (Gomez).

This ancient story told in the *Popol Vuh* shows the power of the gods and reveals a cycle of creation and destruction that has shaped the way the Maya understand time, the divine, and their rulers.

### Humanity in Time

~~The three creations of humanity influenced the Mayas' relationship with time. Because gods destroyed humanity twice before, the Maya beleive the gods could do so again, and because humans were then re-created, the Maya beleive this, too will happen again. These interpretations of the Popol Vuh relate to the Maya belief in time as an endless cycle of beginnings and also is a cycle of endings. To record these never-ending cycles the Mayans invented, "one of the most accurate calendar systems in human history" ("The Calendar System"). The Calendar Round records dates 52 days into the future ("Maya Civilization.").~~

The three creations of humanity, as described in the *Popol Vuh*, have had a great influence on Maya culture, which can be seen in the Maya's relationship with time. Because gods destroyed humanity twice before, the Maya believe the gods could do so again. However, because humans were then re-created, the Maya believe this, too, will happen again. These interpretations of the *Popol Vuh* relate to the Maya belief in time as an endless cycle of beginnings and endings. To record these never-ending cycles of creation and destruction, the Maya invented "one of the most accurate calendar systems in human history" ("The Calendar System"). The Calendar Round records dates 52 days into the future (Mark). The Long Count Calendar, started in 3114 BCE, calculates dates far into the future. The current cycle started in December 2012. This way of timekeeping is still seen in Maya society today. To track the different cycles of

**Skill:
Paraphrasing**

*Josh feels confident that he is paraphrasing information and integrates it selectively in order to maintain the logical flow of ideas and the original meaning of the text. He avoids plagiarism by acknowledging his sources for both paraphrased and quoted material and continues to be sure to include information from more than one source.*

Skill: Critiquing
Research

Josh suspects that by relying primarily on a single source for information, he is missing some deeper understanding of the Maya's relationship with time. He decides to find additional sources. As Josh reads more about the Maya calendar system, he revises and expands his paragraph. He adds information from the new source and revises his discussion. He also realizes he had incorrectly cited one of his sources.

time, Maya communities have "daykeepers." Daykeepers are responsible for keeping the cycles going with the proper rituals and ceremonies. Drawing on centuries of knowledge, they keep track of the calendar, and serve as healers for the Maya people ("The Modern Calendar Priests"). In Maya culture, a calendar is more than a grid or list of dates used for keeping appointments; this calendar encompasses entire life cycles.

According to the Popol Vuh, humanity was created in order to worship the gods. The gods are to be shown respect because they have a lot of power. They have the power to both create and end humanity. The structure of the pyramids is symbolic. The pyramids were built with flat tops. These flat tops created space for rituals. These depictions reveal a belief in life as a series of beginnings and endings.

**The Web of Life**

Thosands of years ago, the Maya first told creation stories in an attempt to understand the world and answering life's big questions, such as, "Who am I?," "Why am I here?," and "Why is the world the way it is?" In answering these questions, the Maya origin stories described the world and beyond as places, "where time is cyclical and all things are interconnected" "Connecting Earth and Sky". These creation stories also describe a special bond between humanity and the gods, as well as a careful balance of creation and destruction, for the Maya who are alive today, these stories serve as an important cultural foundation and are linking it to the past.

### Sources

Spence, Lewis. "The Popol Vuh." *Project Gutenberg.* 1908. http://www.gutenberg.org/files/56550/56550-h/56550-h.htm. Apr. 4, 2018.

"The Calendar System." maya.nmai.si.edu/calendar/calendar-system.

Shumov, Angie. "Creation Myths from Around the World." 2016.

Gomez, Maria C. Ancient History Encyclopedia, "Maya Religion." www.ancient.eu/Maya_Religion/#references.

Gomez, Maria C. "Maya Religion." *Ancient History Encyclopedia*, www.ancient.eu/Maya_Religion/#references. Accessed 8 Apr. 2018.

Jarus, Owen. "The Maya: History, Culture & Religion." *LiveScience*, 22 Aug. 2017, www.livescience.com/41781-the-maya.html. Accessed 9 Apr. 2018.

NOTES

Skill: Sources and Citations

Josh adjusts the style of the website title and adds the date he accessed it to the Gomez citation. He inserts the Jarus citation in his works cited list, including all of the required information. Josh gives proper credit to the sources he uses in his research paper.

Please note that excerpts and passages in the StudySync® library and this workbook are intended as touchstones to generate interest in an author's work. The excerpts and passages do not substitute for the reading of entire texts, and StudySync® strongly recommends that students seek out and purchase the whole literary or informational work in order to experience it as the author intended. Links to online resellers are available in our digital library. In addition, complete works may be ordered through an authorized reseller by filling out and returning to StudySync® the order form enclosed in this workbook.

Reading & Writing Companion  **139**

# Skill:
# Critiquing Research

## ••• CHECKLIST FOR CRITIQUING RESEARCH

In order to conduct short or sustained research projects to answer a question or solve a problem, drawing on several sources, do the following:

- narrow or broaden the question or inquiry as necessary when researching your topic

- synthesize and integrate multiple sources on a subject

- use advanced search terms effectively when looking for information online, such as using unique terms that are specific to your topic (i.e., "daily life in Jamestown, Virginia" rather than just "Jamestown, Virginia")

- assess the usefulness of each source

- integrate information from multiple sources to maintain a flow of ideas

- quote or paraphrase the information without plagiarizing, or copying your source

- provide information about your sources in a works cited list

To evaluate and use relevant information while conducting short or sustained research projects, consider the following questions:

- Have I successfully synthesized and integrated multiple sources on my topic?

- Did I broaden or narrow my research inquiry as needed?

- Are there specific terms or phrases in my research question that I can use to adjust my search?

- Can I use *and, or,* or *not* to expand or limit my search?

- Can I use quotation marks to search for exact phrases?

- Did I quote or paraphrase information without plagiarizing?

- Have I integrated information to maintain a flow of ideas?

- Have I included a works cited list of the sources I have used?

YOUR TURN

Choose the best answer to each question.

1. Below is a section from a previous draft of Josh's research paper. Josh has two sources that discuss the religious significance of Maya pyramids. One source mentions the purpose of the ancient practice of human sacrifice, and one does not. What should Josh do to confirm the reliability of the source in the underlined sentence?

> According to the *Popol Vuh*, the gods created humans because they wanted someone to worship them. Human's submissiveness to the gods is reflected in the design and purpose of Maya pyramids. The structure of the pyramids is deeply symbolic. Each level of a pyramid represents a level of the underworld (Cartwright). <u>At the top of Maya pyramids, rituals of bloodletting and human sacrifice used to be performed for the purpose of returning precious "life force" to the gods (Jarus).</u>

○ A. Cite "Cartwright" as well as "Jarus."

○ B. Josh should trust the source and not worry about it.

○ C. Delete the reference to the purpose of the rituals.

○ D. Check additional sources to confirm the information.

2. Josh critiqued his research process at each step. He began his first draft using the following major research question: How did the origin stories in the *Popol Vuh* shape the ancient Maya's perception of time? As he learned more about the topic, he realized that the Maya still exist today and still practice their religious and cultural beliefs. What should Josh do?

○ A. Modify his research question and revise his research plan.

○ B. Stick with his original research question.

○ C. Reevaluate the validity of his sources.

○ D. Look for additional sources.

 WRITE

Use the questions in the checklist to critique your research process and identify any necessary changes. When you have finished implementing changes to your draft, write out a new version.

Please note that excerpts and passages in the StudySync® library and this workbook are intended as touchstones to generate interest in an author's work. The excerpts and passages do not substitute for the reading of entire texts, and StudySync® strongly recommends that students seek out and purchase the whole literary or informational work in order to experience it as the author intended. Links to online resellers are available in our digital library. In addition, complete works may be ordered through an authorized reseller by filling out and returning to StudySync® the order form enclosed in this workbook.

Reading & Writing Companion 141

# Skill:
# Paraphrasing

## ••• CHECKLIST FOR PARAPHRASING

In order to integrate information into a text, note the following:

- make sure you understand what the author is saying after reading the text carefully
- words and phrases that are important to include in a paraphrase to maintain the meaning of the text
- any words or expressions that are unfamiliar
- avoid plagiarism by acknowledging all sources for both paraphrased and quoted material, as well as over reliance on any one source
- integrate information selectively to maintain a logical flow of ideas

To integrate information into a text, consider the following questions:

- Do I understand the meaning of the text?
- Does my paraphrase of the text maintain its original meaning? Have I missed any key points or details?
- Have I determined the meanings of any words from the text that are unfamiliar to me?
- Did I integrate information selectively to maintain a logical flow of ideas?
- Have I avoided plagiarism by acknowledging all my sources for both paraphrased and quoted material, and avoided over reliance on any one source?

**YOUR TURN**

Josh wants to paraphrase a quotation from the article "The Modern Calendar Priests" in *Archaeology Magazine*. Read the quotation that he wants to paraphrase, and use the checklist on the previous page to answer the multiple-choice questions that follow it.

> "According to Christenson, the Daykeepers' role in the community is to keep track of different cycles of time, to perform the proper rituals to keep the cycles running, and to heal people when they are sick" ("The Modern Calendar Priests").

1. This is an excerpt from a draft of Josh's paper. It shows his first attempt to paraphrase a quotation. What is incorrect about this paraphrasing?

> The current cycle started in December 2012. This way of timekeeping is still seen in Maya society today. "According to Christenson, the Daykeepers' role in the community is to keep track of different cycles of time, to perform the proper rituals to keep the cycles running, and to heal people when they are sick" ("The Modern Calendar Priests").

- A. It is incorrect because it summarizes the information, rather than paraphrasing it.
- B. It is incorrect because it quotes the text directly, rather than paraphrasing it.
- C. It is incorrect because the original meaning of the text is not maintained.
- D. It is incorrect because key points are missing, and this alters the original meaning..

2. What would be the best, most accurate and complete paraphrase of the source?

- A. To track the different cycles of time, Maya communities have "daykeepers." Daykeepers are responsible for keeping the cycles going with the proper rituals and ceremonies ("The Modern Calendar Priests").
- B. The Daykeepers track the different cycles of time and are responsible for keeping up with rituals and ceremonies the community need ("The Modern Calendar Priests").
- C. The Daykeepers are like doctors in that they cure illness and keep time for the community by maintaining the cycles ("The Modern Calendar Priests").
- D. People won't get sick if the rituals perform the cycles and the Daykeepers keep the time correctly ("The Modern Calendar Priests").

✎ **WRITE**

Use the questions in the checklist to paraphrase and integrate a source into a paragraph of your informative research paper. When you have finished, write out the whole paragraph.

# Skill:
# Sources and Citations

## ••• CHECKLIST FOR SOURCES AND CITATIONS

In order to cite and gather relevant information from multiple, authoritative print and digital sources, do the following:

- gather information from a variety of print and digital sources using search terms effectively to narrow your search

- check that sources are useful:

  > find information on authors to see if they are experts on a topic

  > look at the publication date to see if the information is current

  > quote or paraphrase the data you find and cite it to avoid plagiarism, using parenthetical citations, footnotes, or endnotes to credit sources

- integrate information from various sources selectively to maintain a logical flow of ideas in the text, using transitional words and phrases

- include all sources in a bibliography or works cited list, following a standard format:

  > Halall, Ahmed. *The Pyramids of Ancient Egypt.* Central Publishing, 2016.

  > for a citation, footnote, or endnote, include the author, title, and page number

To check that sources are gathered and cited correctly, consider the following questions:

- Did I cite the information I found using a standard format to avoid plagiarism?

- Have I relied on one source, instead of looking for different points of view on my topic in other sources?

- Did I include all my sources in my bibliography or works cited list?

**YOUR TURN**

Choose the best answer to each question.

1. Below is a section from a previous draft of Josh's research paper. In it, he cites a printed book he read about origin stories. What change should Josh make to improve the clarity of his citations?

> In the introduction to her book *Primal Myths,* religion professor Barbara C. Sproul says that creation myths helped humans explain "first causes" and provided a way for humans to "organize the way we perceive facts and understand ourselves in the world" (Sproul). The Maya were one such ancient culture.

- ○ A. Delete Sproul's name from the parentheses following the quotation.
- ○ B. Add the page number in the parentheses following the quotation.
- ○ C. Add the title of the book to the parentheses following the quotation.
- ○ D. No change needs to be made.

2. Below is a section from a previous draft of Josh's works cited list. Which revision best corrects his style errors?

> Boyd, Mildred. "The Modern Maya." *Mexico's Culture and History,* www.chapala.com/chapala/magnificentmexico/modernmaya/modernmaya.html.

- ○ A. www.chapala.com/chapala/magnificentmexico/modernmaya/modernmaya.html. Accessed Dec. 13, 2018. Boyd, Mildred. The Modern Maya." *Mexico's Culture and History.*
- ○ B. Boyd, Mildred. *Mexico's Culture and History,* "The Modern Maya." www.chapala.com/chapala/magnificentmexico/modernmaya/modernmaya.html.
- ○ C. Mildred Boyd. "The Modern Maya." *Mexico's Culture and History,* www.chapala.com/chapala/magnificentmexico/modernmaya/modernmaya.html.
- ○ D. Boyd, Mildred. "The Modern Maya." *Mexico's Culture and History,* www.chapala.com/chapala/magnificentmexico/modernmaya/modernmaya.html. Accessed 13 Dec. 2018.

 **WRITE**

Use the questions in the checklist to revise your academic citations and works cited list of source materials for your research paper. When you have finished revising your sources and citations, write out a new copy.

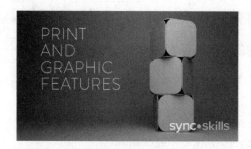

# Skill:
# Print and Graphic Features

## ••• CHECKLIST FOR PRINT AND GRAPHIC FEATURES

First, reread your draft and ask yourself the following questions:

- To what extent would including formatting, graphics, or multimedia be effective in achieving my purpose?
- Which formatting, graphics, or multimedia seem most important for conveying information to the reader?
- How is the addition of the formatting, graphics, or multimedia useful to aiding comprehension?

To include formatting, graphics, and multimedia, use the following questions as a guide:

- How can I use formatting to better organize information? Consider adding:

  > titles

  > headings

  > subheadings

  > bullets

  > boldface and italicized terms

How can I use graphics to better convey information? Consider adding:

  > charts, graphs, and/or tables

  > timelines, diagrams, and/or maps

How can I use multimedia to add interest and variety? Consider adding a combination of the following, including captions:

  > photographs

  > art

  > audio

  > video

Copyright © BookheadEd Learning, LLC

## ⟳ YOUR TURN

Choose the best answer to each question.

1. Reread the paragraph from a previous draft of Josh's research paper. Which of the following headings best represents the content of the passage and would help his audience focus on the main idea?

> Thousands of years ago, the Maya first told creation stories in an attempt to understand the world and to answer life's big questions, such as "Who am I?," "Why am I here?," and "Why is the world the way it is?" In attempting to answer these questions, the Maya origin stories described the world and beyond as places "where time is cyclical and all things are interconnected" ("Connecting Earth and Sky"). In other words, time is an intricately woven web that connects all beings and events. These creation stories also describe a special bond between humanity and the gods, as well as a careful balance of creation and destruction. For the Maya who are alive today, these stories serve as an important cultural foundation and link to the past. For the world, links to ancient cultures can serve as guideposts: no matter what the future holds, human beings must find a way, as the Daykeepers did, to adjust their settings and keep on going.

○ A. Questions of Life
○ B. The Web of Life
○ C. Balancing Creations and Destruction
○ D. The Daykeepers

2. Josh also considers adding an image, graph, or table to help his audience understand the Maya creation story. Which of the following graphic elements would be most helpful for readers?

○ A. An image of a web as a series of cycles.
○ B. A timeline showing the calendar of the Maya.
○ C. A graphic displaying the various types of humans created by the Mayan gods.
○ D. An image showing Mayan ruins with carvings that show the cycle of life.

## ✏ WRITE

Use the questions in the checklist to add at least three headings, two graphics, and one piece of multimedia to your research paper. When you have finished revising your draft, write out a new copy.

Please note that excerpts and passages in the StudySync® library and this workbook are intended as touchstones to generate interest in an author's work. The excerpts and passages do not substitute for the reading of entire texts, and StudySync® strongly recommends that students seek out and purchase the whole literary or informational work in order to experience it as the author intended. Links to online resellers are available in our digital library. In addition, complete works may be ordered through an authorized reseller by filling out and returning to StudySync® the order form enclosed in this workbook.

Reading & Writing Companion  147

# Research Writing Process: Revise

| PLAN | DRAFT | REVISE | EDIT AND PUBLISH |

You have written a draft of your research paper. You have also received input from your peers about how to improve it. Now you are going to revise your draft.

## ◄ REVISION GUIDE

Examine your draft to find areas for revision. Use the guide below to help you review:

| Review | Revise | Example |
|---|---|---|
| **Clarity** | | |
| Identify difficult concepts or complex quoted language in your research paper. Annotate places in which additional explanation or clarification might be helpful to readers. | Follow challenging material with a restatement in simpler terms to assist your audience's understanding. | In attempting to answering these questions, the Maya origin stories described the world and beyond as places "where time is cyclical and all things are interconnected" ("Connecting Earth and Sky"). In other words, time is like an intricately woven web that connects all beings and events. |

| Review | Revise | Example |
|--------|--------|---------|
| **Development** | | |
| Synthesize key ideas from multiple sources. Annotate places where additional description or information could help develop your ideas. | Integrate quoted material with paraphrased material, avoiding over-reliance on one source of information. Use commas and other punctuation for clarification. Cite all sources. | Finally, on the third attempt, the gods "made four men out of white and yellow corn" and were satisfied that "these men could think and feel and speak words out of love and respect" (Shumov). In Maria Gomez's retelling, these humans were actually "too wise." Rather than destroy the human race for a third time, however, one of the gods "clouded their minds and eyes so they would become less wise" (Gomez). |
| **Organization** | | |
| Review your writing for opportunities to use print features to clarify information. | Add transitions to connect information across paragraphs. Use bulleted lists to break down information or sequence complex information to enhance reader comprehension. Include citations. | For centuries, the *Popol Vuh* has shaped Mayan understanding of life as a cycel. The story begins with the gods gathering to create the earth. After building the world, the gods wanted to fill it with creatures who would worship them (Shumov). <br> • First, they created humans from wet clay, but these humans could not speak, so the gods destroyed them in a flood. <br> • On their second attempt, the gods created humans out of wood; however, as Shumov explains, while these humans could talk, "they were empty headed and empty hearted." So, the gods destroyed the human race a second time. |

Please note that excerpts and passages in the StudySync® library and this workbook are intended as touchstones to generate interest in an author's work. The excerpts and passages do not substitute for the reading of entire texts, and StudySync® strongly recommends that students seek out and purchase the whole literary or informational work in order to experience it as the author intended. Links to online resellers are available in our digital library. In addition, complete works may be ordered through an authorized reseller by filling out and returning to StudySync® the order form enclosed in this workbook.

Reading & Writing Companion

149

| Review | Revise | Example |
|--------|--------|---------|
| **Style: Word Choice** | | |
| Identify weak or repetitive words or phrases that do not clearly or precisely express your ideas to the reader. | Replace weak and repetitive words and phrases with more descriptive or precise ones that better convey your ideas. | The gods are to be ~~shown~~ respected because they ~~have a lot of power. They~~ have the power to both create and ~~end~~ destroy humanity. |
| **Style: Sentence Effectiveness** | | |
| Read your research paper aloud. Annotate places where you have too many short sentences in a row. Using relative pronouns to link closely related sentences or independent clauses can add clarity by associating ideas. Vary your sentence beginnings. | Combine short sentences that are closely related by linking them together using relative pronouns. Add details that provide more complete information. | The structure of the pyramids is symbolic. For example, the ~~The~~ pyramids were built with flat tops. ~~These flat tops,~~ which created space ~~for~~ on which rituals. ~~The rituals~~ of bloodletting and human sacrifice were performed to honor the gods by returning "life force" to the gods (Jarus). |

## ✏ WRITE

Use the guide above, as well as your peer reviews, to help you evaluate your research paper to determine areas that should be revised.

# Skill:
# Using a Style Guide

## ••• CHECKLIST FOR USING A STYLE GUIDE

In order to write your work so that it conforms to the guidelines in a style manual, do the following:

- When doing research, keep careful bibliographic notes (type of work, publishing information, location of information) on each source you use and the information you will cite from that source.

- Determine which style guide (e.g., *MLA Handbook*, *Turabian's Manual for Writers*) you should use *before* you write your draft.

  > Follow the choice as directed by a teacher or assignment requirements.

  > Familiarize yourself with that guide and check your writing against the guide when you edit.

- As you draft, write in-text citations following the style guide.

- Once your draft has been revised, compile your works cited list or bibliography following the style of the chosen guide. The guide is organized by type of source—book, magazine, newspaper, website—number of authors (if known), and other relevant bibliographic data.

To edit your work so that it conforms to the guidelines in a style manual, consider the following questions:

- Have I followed the conventions for spelling, punctuation, capitalization, sentence structure, and formatting according to the style guide?

- Does each in-text citation conform to the style guide?

- Do I have an entry in my works cited list or bibliography for each reference used?

- Have I followed the correct style, including capitalization and punctuation, for each entry?

Please note that excerpts and passages in the StudySync® library and this workbook are intended as touchstones to generate interest in an author's work. The excerpts and passages do not substitute for the reading of entire texts, and StudySync® strongly recommends that students seek out and purchase the whole literary or informational work in order to experience it as the author intended. Links to online resellers are available in our digital library. In addition, complete works may be ordered through an authorized reseller by filling out and returning to StudySync® the order form enclosed in this workbook.

Reading & Writing
Companion

**151**

## ⟳ YOUR TURN

Read the types of information below. Then, complete the chart by sorting them into those that are found in a style guide and those that are not.

| Types of Information | | | |
|---|---|---|---|
| **A** | how to cite Internet sources | **F** | how to write an outline |
| **B** | synonyms for a word | **G** | how to format a bibliography |
| **C** | a list of possible research topics | **H** | the definition of a word |
| **D** | when to use italics | **I** | how to select a thesis |
| **E** | proper punctuation for quotations | **J** | when to use a hyphen |

| In a Style Guide | Not in a Style Guide |
|---|---|
|  |  |
|  |  |
|  |  |
|  |  |
|  |  |

## ✏ WRITE

Use the checklist to help you choose a convention that has been problematic for you. Use a credible style guide to check and correct any errors related to that convention in your research paper.

# Grammar: Conjunctive Adverbs

## Conjunctive Adverb

A conjunctive adverb is a special kind of adverb that is used to connect related ideas in two different sentences. Conjunctive adverbs are usually more formal than coordinating conjunctions.

| Use | Examples |
|---|---|
| to replace *and* | also, besides, furthermore, moreover |
| to replace *but* | however, nevertheless, still, instead |
| to show cause and effect | consequently, therefore, thus |
| to compare or contrast | equally, likewise, similarly, conversely |
| to state an opinion | fortunately, unfortunately, ironically |
| to reinforce an argument | certainly, indeed |
| to show order of time | subsequently, afterwards, then |

Conjunctive adverbs are used to join two independent clauses. Usually, a semicolon separates the two clauses and a comma follows the conjunctive adverb. The conjunctive adverb clarifies the relationship between the two ideas in the clauses.

| Correct | Incorrect |
|---|---|
| Many theories now accepted by science were once scorned; **therefore**, we should be careful not to dismiss any new theory too quickly. | Many theories now accepted by science were once scorned; likewise, we should be careful not to dismiss any new theory too quickly. |

## ⟳ YOUR TURN

1. How should this sentence be changed?

> The plays of Sophocles and Euripides entertained and enlightened the audiences of ancient Greece; instead, they are still being performed today.

○ A. Replace the semicolon with a comma.

○ B. Replace **instead** with **moreover**.

○ C. Replace **instead** with **therefore**.

○ D. No change needs to be made to this sentence.

2. How should this sentence be changed?

> A common theme in stories about war is how fighting changes the soldier; consequently, the same stories often stress how the fighting does not change the military situation.

○ A. Replace **consequently** with **ironically**.

○ B. Replace **consequently** with **subsequently**.

○ C. Replace **consequently** with **fortunately**.

○ D. No change needs to be made to this sentence.

3. How should this sentence be changed?

> In *Animal Farm*, George Orwell analyzes how power develops within a society; unfortunately, Orwell's tale demonstrates that society's members are partly responsible for their own powerlessness.

○ A. Replace **unfortunately** with **so**.

○ B. Replace **unfortunately** with **instead**.

○ C. Replace **unfortunately** with **conversely**.

○ D. No change needs to be made to this sentence.

4. How should this sentence be changed?

> Personal electronic communication, which can be tracked, will completely transform commerce and politics; nevertheless, there are already ways to monitor the hashtags that appear in social media.

○ A. Replace **nevertheless** with **however**.

○ B. Replace **nevertheless** with **therefore**.

○ C. Replace **nevertheless** with **indeed**.

○ D. No change needs to be made to this sentence.

# Grammar: Commonly Misspelled Words

By following a few simple steps, you can learn to spell new words—even words that are unfamiliar or difficult. As you write, keep a list of words you have trouble spelling. Refer to online or print resources for pronunciation, Latin or Greek roots, and other information that may help you. Then use the steps below to learn to spell those words.

**Say it.** Look at the word again and say it aloud. Say it again, pronouncing each syllable clearly.

**See it.** Close your eyes. Picture the word. Visualize it letter by letter.

**Write it.** Look at the word again and write it two or three times. Then write the word without looking at the printed version.

**Check it.** Check your spelling. Did you spell it correctly? If not, repeat each step until you can spell it easily.

Here are some words that can sometimes confuse even strong spellers.

| Commonly Misspelled Words | | |
| --- | --- | --- |
| abdomen | acquaintance | admission |
| advertisement | aerial | bibliography |
| bureaucrat | coming | cataclysm |
| colonel | concede | conscientious |
| discrimination | dissatisfaction | forfeit |
| gauge | grammatically | hindrance |
| ingenious | livelihood | luxurious |
| marriageable | mathematics | negotiable |
| parliament | personnel | significant |
| succession | twelfth | variety |

## ⟳ YOUR TURN

1.  How should this sentence be changed?

> When buraucrat Mike Smithson revealed his sources, the rest of the members were stunned by the admision.

○  A.  Change **buraucrat** to **bureaucrat** and **admision** to **admission**.
○  B.  Change **buraucrat** to **buracrat** and **admision** to **admition**.
○  C.  Change **buraucrat** to **buraecrat** and **admision** to **admition**.
○  D.  No change needs to be made to this sentence.

2.  How should this sentence be changed?

> At that point, most of the members were forced to consede that Smithson's revelation was a signifacant one.

○  A.  Change **consede** to **conscede** and **signifacant** to **significent**.
○  B.  Change **consede** to **concede** and **signifacant** to **significant**.
○  C.  Change **consede** to **conceed** and **signifacant** to **singnifigant**.
○  D.  No change needs to be made to this sentence.

3.  How should this sentence be changed?

> Melanie was amazed by the huge variety of the sources she found in the bibliografy of her chemistry textbook.

○  A.  Change **variety** to **vareity**.
○  B.  Change **bibliografy** to **bibliography**.
○  C.  Change **variety** to **varietie** and **bibliografy** to **bibbliografy**.
○  D.  No change needs to be made to this sentence.

4.  How should this sentence be changed?

> It was impossible to gauge the full extent of the damage, but many people called last week's hurricane a cataclysm.

○  A.  Change **gauge** to **guage**.
○  B.  Change **cataclysm** to **cataclism**.
○  C.  Change **gauge** to **gage** and **cataclysm** to **cateclysm**.
○  D.  No change needs to be made to this sentence.

# Research Writing Process: Edit and Publish

| PLAN | DRAFT | REVISE | EDIT AND PUBLISH |
|------|-------|--------|------------------|

You have revised your research paper based on your peer feedback and your own examination.

Now, it is time to edit your research paper. When you revised, you focused on the content of your research paper. You probably critiqued your research process and carefully evaluated your sources and citations. When you edit, you focus on the mechanics of your research paper, paying close attention to things like grammar and punctuation.

**Use the checklist below to guide you as you edit:**

☐ Have I used commas correctly to set off source material?

☐ Have I used parallel construction?

☐ Have I avoided misusing commas that result in comma splices?

☐ Do I have any sentence fragments or run-on sentences?

☐ Have I used conjunctive adverbs correctly, with or without a semicolon?

☐ Have I spelled everything correctly?

**Notice some edits Josh has made:**

- Added a comma after an introductory phrase.

- Edited text to make two sections parallel.

- Replaced a comma with a period to avoid a comma splice.

- Deleted an unnecessary comma before a quotation.

- Added parentheses around an in-text citation.

- Added a conjunctive adverb to create transition.

- Corrected two spelling errors.

Please note that excerpts and passages in the StudySync® library and this workbook are intended as touchstones to generate interest in an author's work. The excerpts and passages do not substitute for the reading of entire texts, and StudySync® strongly recommends that students seek out and purchase the whole literary or informational work in order to experience it as the author intended. Links to online resellers are available in our digital library. In addition, complete works may be ordered through an authorized reseller by filling out and returning to StudySync® the order form enclosed in this workbook.

Reading & Writing Companion

**157**

~~Thosands~~ Thousands of years ago, the Maya first told creation stories in an attempt to understand the world and ~~answering~~ to answer life's big questions, such as~~,~~ "Who am I?," "Why am I here?," and "Why is the world the way it is?" In attempting to answer these questions, the Maya origin stories described the world and beyond as places "where time is cyclical and all things are interconnected" ("Connecting Earth and Sky"). . . . These creation stories also describe a special bond between ~~humanty~~ humanity and the gods, as well as a careful balance of creation and destruction~~,~~. ~~for~~ Indeed, for the Maya who are alive today, these stories serve as an important cultural foundation and ~~are linking it~~ a link to the past.

## ✏ WRITE

Use the questions above, as well as your peer reviews, to help you evaluate your research paper to determine areas that need editing. Then edit your research paper to correct those errors.

Once you have made all your corrections, you are ready to publish your work. You can distribute your writing to family and friends, hang it on a bulletin board, or post it on your blog. If you publish online, share the link with your family, friends, and classmates.

# Tiger Moms and Trophies for Everyone

INFORMATIONAL TEXT

## Introduction

Tiger Mom Amy Chua faced a lot of criticism for her parenting style. But is parenting one-size-fits-all? Or do different cultural groups have their own traditions and values to uphold as parents?

## V VOCABULARY

### approach
a method or technique

### culture
the beliefs, customs, and practices that distinguish one group or society from another

### conflict
a serious disagreement or argument

### obedience
compliance or submission to another's authority

### controversial
causing disagreement or debate

NOTES

## ☰ READ

1    Parenting is a **controversial** topic. People have many different ideas about the best way to raise kids. Parenting strategies include free-range parenting, helicopter parenting, tiger parenting, and elephant parenting. Amy Chua, known as the tiger mom, faced criticism when she wrote about her **approach** to parenting. Chua acknowledges that while her parenting style is common among Chinese parents, it may seem harsh to people who are familiar with a more Western parenting style. After excerpts from her book were published online, many people challenged her for demanding perfection from her daughters. Looking carefully at both sides of the issue can be helpful before deciding who is right.

2    In Chinese **culture**, each year on the lunar calendar has its own animal sign. Chua was born during the year of the tiger, and she explains that the tiger is a symbol of authority. For Chua, being Chinese means that her parenting style is not just a personal choice. She says that Chinese culture values **obedience**. As a Chinese tiger mom, she expects her daughters to obey her rules. These rules include not being allowed to watch TV or play video games and not being allowed to perform in a school play. She forces her daughters

to practice violin and piano for hours every day. She expects them to get straight As on every report card. Chua argues that many Chinese parents think that being strict and having the highest standards for their children prepares them for the future. They believe that this style of parenting gives kids confidence and strong work habits.

3   Chua's parenting style has its roots in the Chinese cultural tradition of filial piety, or respect for elders. The rule of filial piety says that you must respect and obey people who are older than you, especially your parents. A collection of folktales from around the 13th century, *The Twenty-Four Stories of Filial Piety*, gives examples of filial sons putting their parents' needs before their own. In one story, Jiang Ge carries his mother on his back to his cousin's village. Once they arrive in his cousin's village, Jiang Ge has lost his clothes and shoes. Without clothes or shoes, he starts working to support his mother. Other stories show children obeying their parents' wishes even when their parents are unkind. In one example, Wang Xiang's father and stepmother are cruel to him. His stepmother likes to eat fish, but the river is frozen solid in winter. Wang Xiang lies down on the ice to melt it with his body. Once the ice melts, he catches fresh fish to serve his stepmother. Filial piety is an important Chinese cultural value, and parents like Chua honor their cultural roots by keeping these traditions alive.

4   As an alternative to tiger parenting and its focus on respect for elders, Western parenting styles often prioritize the well-being of the child. Researchers at the University of Arizona report that Western parents tend to give kids positive support and set moderate expectations. According to their research, this kind of parenting is healthy for kids. Parents who follow a Western model are more likely to worry about kids' self-esteem, and their family culture is warmer and more affectionate.

5   But is it possible to worry too much about kids' self-esteem? Can anti-tiger parenting have negative effects too? A growing trend among Western parents is to give awards to all the kids who participate in an event, not just the winners. Supporters of this practice say that children should be rewarded for their efforts no matter the outcome. They say that they are protecting kids' feelings. But others argue that handing out trophies to all participants in a sports tournament, for example, sends kids the wrong message. Instead of preparing them for the real world where not everyone is a winner, this practice teaches kids that they can be rewarded for just showing up.

6   The Western parenting model does focus more on the child's self-image, but these children may not be prepared to deal with **conflict** and challenges. They might not have skills to cope with disappointment or rejection. Evaluating both sides helps consider the details before deciding who is right.

Please note that excerpts and passages in the StudySync® library and this workbook are intended as touchstones to generate interest in an author's work. The excerpts and passages do not substitute for the reading of entire texts, and StudySync® strongly recommends that students seek out and purchase the whole literary or informational work in order to experience it as the author intended. Links to online resellers are available in our digital library. In addition, complete works may be ordered through an authorized reseller by filling out and returning to StudySync® the order form enclosed in this workbook.

Reading & Writing Companion   **161**

An obedient son in *The Twenty-Four Stories of Filial Piety* strangles a tiger to protect his father from being attacked.

Jiang Ge carries his mother on his back.

Wang Xiang melts ice with his body and catches a fish for his stepmother.

Reading & Writing Companion

# First Read

Read "Tiger Moms and Trophies for Everyone: How Culture Influences Parenting." After you read, complete the Think Questions below.

## ☁ THINK QUESTIONS

1. What are some of the rules that Amy Chua, the tiger mom, expects her daughters to follow?

   Tiger mom Amy Chua's rules include _____

   _____.

2. What is the Chinese cultural tradition of filial piety?

   In the tradition of filial piety, children must _____.

3. What are some examples of filial piety? Include textual evidence to support your response.

   One example of filial piety is _____.

   The text says " _____."

4. Use context to confirm the meaning of the word *obedience* as it is used in "Tiger Moms and Trophies for Everyone." Write your definition of *obedience* here.

   *Obedience* means _____.

   A context clue is _____.

5. What is another way to say that a topic is *controversial*?

   The topic is _____.

Please note that excerpts and passages in the StudySync® library and this workbook are intended as touchstones to generate interest in an author's work. The excerpts and passages do not substitute for the reading of entire texts, and StudySync® strongly recommends that students seek out and purchase the whole literary or informational work in order to experience it as the author intended. Links to online resellers are available in our digital library. In addition, complete works may be ordered through an authorized reseller by filling out and returning to StudySync® the order form enclosed in this workbook.

Reading & Writing Companion    163

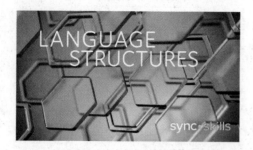

# Skill:
# Language Structures

## ★ DEFINE

In every language, there are rules that tell how to **structure** sentences. These rules define the correct order of words. In the English language, for example, a **basic** structure for sentences is subject, verb, and object. Some sentences have more **complicated** structures.

You will encounter both basic and complicated **language structures** in the classroom materials you read. Being familiar with language structures will help you better understand the text.

## ••• CHECKLIST FOR LANGUAGE STRUCTURES

To improve your comprehension of language structures, do the following:

 Monitor your understanding.

- Ask yourself: Why do I not understand this sentence? Is it because the sentence is long? Or is it because I do not understand the logical relationship between the ideas in this sentence?

- Pay attention to coordinating conjunctions.

  > **Coordinating conjunctions** show an equal emphasis on the ideas in a sentence.

  > The coordinating conjunction *and* shows that two or more things are true of a person, object, or event.
  Example: Josefina is a good athlete **and** student.

  > The coordinating conjunction *or* shows a choice between different possibilities.
  Example: Josefina can either do her homework **or** go for a run.

  > The coordinating conjunction *but* shows a contrast between people, objects, or events.
  Example: Josefina wants to run **but** should finish her homework first.

- Break down the sentence into its parts.

  > Ask yourself: what ideas are expressed in this sentence? Are there conjunctions that join ideas or show contrast?

✓ Confirm your understanding with a peer or teacher.

## ↻ YOUR TURN

Read the following excerpt from paragraph 3 of "Tiger Moms and Trophies for Everyone." Then, using the Checklist on the previous page, answer the multiple-choice questions below.

---

**from "Tiger Moms and Trophies for Everyone"**

(1) In one example, Wang Xiang's father and stepmother are cruel to him. (2) His stepmother likes to eat fish, but the river is frozen solid in winter. (3) Wang Xiang lays down on the ice to melt it with his body. (4) Once the ice melts, he catches fresh fish to serve his stepmother. (5) Filial piety is an important Chinese cultural value, and parents like Chua honor their cultural roots by keeping these traditions alive.

---

1. Which sentences use coordinating conjunctions?

   ○ A. sentences 2 and 3
   ○ B. sentences 3 and 4
   ○ C. sentences 2 and 5
   ○ D. sentences 4 and 5

2. What is the subordinating conjunction in sentence 4?

   ○ A. once
   ○ B. melts
   ○ C. to
   ○ D. he

3. What is true about the clauses in sentence 5?

   ○ A. The first clause is more important than the second.
   ○ B. The second clause is more important than the first.
   ○ C. The clauses are both subordinate.
   ○ D. The clauses are equally important.

# Skill: Visual and Contextual Support

## ★ DEFINE

**Visual support** is an image or an object that helps you understand a text. **Contextual support** is a **feature** that helps you understand a text. By using visual and contextual supports, you can develop your vocabulary so you can better understand a variety of texts.

First, preview the text to identify any visual supports. These might include illustrations, graphics, charts, or other objects in a text. Then, identify any contextual supports. Examples of contextual supports are titles, headers, captions, and boldface terms. Write down your **observations**.

Then, write down what those visual and contextual supports tell you about the meaning of the text. Note any new vocabulary that you see in those supports. Ask your peers and your teacher to **confirm** your understanding of the text.

## ••• CHECKLIST FOR VISUAL AND CONTEXTUAL SUPPORT

To use visual and contextual support to understand texts, do the following:

- ✓ Preview the text. Read the title, headers, and other features. Look at any images and graphics.

- ✓ Write down the visual and contextual supports in the text.

- ✓ Write down what those supports tell you about the text.

- ✓ Note any new vocabulary that you see in those supports.

- ✓ Create an illustration for the reading and write a descriptive caption.

- ✓ Confirm your observations with your peers and teacher.

**YOUR TURN**

Read each example of visual and contextual supports below. Then, complete the chart by sorting them into those that are visual supports and those that are contextual supports.

| Visual and Contextual Supports | |
|---|---|
| **A.** the title of a scientific study | **E.** an infographic about immigration to America |
| **B.** a boldface vocabulary word | **F.** headers dividing an article into sections |
| **C.** a sketch of a main character | **G.** a photograph of an author |
| **D.** a pie chart showing a state's budget | **H.** a caption that describes an image |

| Visual Supports | Contextual Supports |
|---|---|
| | |
| | |
| | |
| | |

Please note that excerpts and passages in the StudySync® library and this workbook are intended as touchstones to generate interest in an author's work. The excerpts and passages do not substitute for the reading of entire texts, and StudySync® strongly recommends that students seek out and purchase the whole literary or informational work in order to experience it as the author intended. Links to online resellers are available in our digital library. In addition, complete works may be ordered through an authorized reseller by filling out and returning to StudySync® the order form enclosed in this workbook.

Reading & Writing Companion 167

# Close Read

---

### ✏ WRITE

INFORMATIVE:  Think about the different parenting styles presented in "Tiger Moms and Trophies for Everyone" and about other parenting styles that you have experienced or learned about. Write a paragraph that explains how families' cultural backgrounds influence their parenting styles. Support your conclusions with details and evidence from the text and from your own knowledge and personal experiences. Pay attention to and edit for the formation of plural nouns.

**Use the checklist below to guide you as you write.**

☐ What does "Tiger Moms and Trophies for Everyone" explain about culture and parenting?

☐ What have you seen in your own family or community that connects cultural values with parenting styles?

☐ How do you think culture influences parenting styles?

**Use the sentence frames to organize and write your informational response.**

Families' cultural backgrounds influence their parenting styles because parents pass on their families'

_____,

customs, and practices. For example, Amy Chua's parenting style is influenced by _____.

In my experience, parents get ideas about the best way to raise kids from their _____.

For example, my _____ believes in _____.

I know that _____ influenced (his / her) parenting style.

---

# Karima

### FICTION

## Introduction

Karima's life as an immigrant is complicated—she constantly faces the expectations of everyone around her, including her parents, her Arabic school friends, and her American high school peers. Can she maintain an independent sense of herself as she navigates through awkward social situations, encounters prejudice toward Arabs, and deals with the feelings of being misunderstood?

## VOCABULARY

**assimilate**

to fully become part of the culture of a population or group

**subtle**

not obvious

**culture**

a group's beliefs, customs, and social behavior that separate them from another group

NO
IMAGE
PROVIDED

**xenophobia**

the fear or dislike of people from other countries

VOTE

**exercise**

to use or implement

NOTES

## READ

CHARACTERS:
Karima, 15
Karima's Mom, 40
Karima's Dad, 45
Sarah, 15
Malcolm, 16
Rabia, 15
Ahmed, 15

**Scene 1** - Karima's home.

1 *Karima and her parents are in spirited but friendly discussion. They are having tea and bread in the family's living room. Because this play happens in Karima's own head—from her point of view—she occasionally addresses the audience with comments/asides. Karima's parents speak English with strong Levantine Arabic accents. Karima speaks English with a slight accent.*

2    KARIMA

It's absolutely ridiculous! "Go back to where you come from"?! I mean, HELLO, she's from Dallas! She was born here. Just because she covers her head, just because she's Muslim!

3    KARIMA'S MOM

(shaking her head)
It's terrible, I know. I'm so proud of you for sticking beside your friend. *That's who we are.*

4    KARIMA

Of course I did. And you know what? I'm thinking of starting to wear my hijab to school, too, like Rabia—

5    KARIMA'S MOM

No, Karima, don't be silly, why do that?

6    KARIMA

Why not? Why do I wear it everywhere else then? It seems like I'm trying to make them feel comfortable instead of **exercising** my right in this country!

7    KARIMA'S DAD

People are afraid of what they don't understand. Every time they talk about us on the news it's with the word *terrorist* attached—*Arab terrorist*—and this naturally leads to violence. But I agree with your mother. You shouldn't call attention to yourself at school. It's important to **assimilate**, to get along—

8    KARIMA'S MOM

Yes! it's okay to want to fit in, Karima. It's okay to have an American high school experience while keeping close to your Palestinian identity and family.

9    KARIMA

(to audience, rolls eyes)
Thanks, Mom, why didn't / think of that?
(back to scene)
But I'm proud of our **culture**, why should I have to hide it?

10    KARIMA'S DAD

It's not about hiding, Karima! It's about being comfortable with anyone, anywhere. The most important thing is your—

11    KARIMA

My education, I know.
(to the audience)

The thing about parents is that they're the same everywhere: they repeat the same things over and over like you're deaf or something. . .

12   KARIMA'S MOM

We're so proud of you. The world needs more brilliant women going into STEM fields. You're an exceptional student. In the end, that's what matters most.

13   KARIMA'S DAD

Yes, it's undoubtedly difficult to be a target of **xenophobia** in your own country, as a contributing citizen! But at the same time, you, Karima, with hard work, are going to be able to be and do anything you want. *Anything. (holding back tears)* That is why we're here.

14   KARIMA

(to audience)

Oh no, this is where he starts tearing up. I'm grateful, I really am, but it makes me uncomfortable when he starts talking about everything they sacrificed for me. It's a lot of pressure.

15   KARIMA'S DAD

(suddenly stern, a warning)

As long as you remember that the most important thing is your—

16   KARIMA

(to audience)

Say it with me now. . .Wait for it. . ."Education!"

17   KARIMA'S MOM

You're not getting bullied are you?

18   KARIMA

No, at school they just think I'm weird and nerdy. It's like I'm not American enough for high school, but I'm also not Arab enough for my Arab friends. It's like I don't quite fit anywhere. . .

19   KARIMA'S DAD

Pffff. Don't let anyone tell you who you are. You're my Karima. You're perfect, exactly as you are.

20   KARIMA

(to audience)

First of all, my dad is not *always* so cool. Sometimes he doesn't think I'm so perfect when I bring home less than a perfect grade, for example. Second, I wouldn't tell my parents because they'd worry, but it still *feels* like I'm being bullied even though I can't point to one big thing. It's way more **subtle** than having GO BACK TO WHERE YOU CAME FROM spray painted on your locker, like what happened to Rabia today. She couldn't help but cry in the hallway, in front of everyone. That's what she said hurt her the most when we finally got to be alone at her house. She just didn't want them to see her cry. But she just couldn't help it. So I guess I shouldn't complain because everyone's kind of nice to me. But they ask so many questions like I'm a zoo animal. And all the questions make me want to hide in my books and shut the world out. But, I guess, maybe that's partly why I'm so smart? (Laughs at herself) And also modest, of course. Oh no, I'm late for school. . .

21 *Karima runs to the other side of the stage into. . .*

**Scene 2** - *A public high school in Texas. Karima is getting books out of her locker, when two classmates, SARAH and COURTNEY, approach her. They're overly friendly.*

22 SARAH
Hey Ka. . .um. . .

23 KARIMA
Karima.

24 SARAH
I knew that!

25 COURTNEY
Karina, right. See? I *told* you.

26 KARIMA
No, it's actually Karima, with an m.

27 SARAH
SO cute! Where is that name from? My name is SO BORING. Sarah. Barf.

28 COURTNEY
Mine toooo! Courtney is just like. . .blah. Bored. So where are you from again?

29 KARIMA
I'm from, my family's from Palestine. My name means generous in Arabic.

30 SARAH
Wow. That's *crazy.* And your accent is *adorbs.*

31 KARIMA
Um. . .ok?

NOTES

**32  COURTNEY**

So we were just wondering if you wanted to hang out with us this weekend? Like, wanna go to the game with us? We pre-game at Dan's house, it's really fun and chill.

**33  SARAH**

Ok fine we'll tell you!! But top secret, ok? Full disclosure: our friend who also happens to be my second cousin and *really* good friend Ben has a *massive* crush on you. So we're asking for him.

**34  COURTNEY**

Not that we don't wanna hang, too.

**35  SARAH**

Oh duh definitely want to hang! But Ben's been asking us. . .

**36  KARIMA**

(turning bright red)

Really? Wow. That sounds fun. . .

**37  SARAH & COURTNEY**

SO FUN!!

**38  KARIMA**

(realizing, backtracking)

But, actually, I'm not really allowed to go to the games, or out on weekends. I mean, I would, I just. . .can't. Sorry. But thanks for inviting me.

**39  SARAH**

Tragic. What do you do on weekends then!?

**40  KARIMA**

(unsure, doesn't want to say)

Um. . .family stuff, mostly.

**41  SARAH**

Wow is that like an Arab thing?

**42  COURTNEY**

Where *is* Palestine, exactly? Like what language do you speak?

**43  SARAH & COURTNEY IN UNISON, GROWING IN SPEED AND VOLUME**

What do you eat there? Do you eat the same stuff here? Why did you leave? Why does your friend wear a scarf on her head? What does it mean? Do your parents wear weird stuff too? Do Arabs like Americans? Do you know any terrorists? Are you religious?

44   *Karima turns to the audience, shuts her eyes tight and covers her ears and SCREAMS. The voices and characters disappear. BLACK OUT.*

**Scene 3** - *Outside of Karima's Arabic School, Saturday afternoon*

45   *Karima with her two closest Arabic school friends, Rabia and Ahmed. They walk and talk as they hit the sidewalk. All three speak to each other in Arabic, with a few English words thrown in. Rabia and Karima both have their heads covered.*

46   KARIMA
(in Arabic)
Ok, should we go to Ahmed's?

47   RABIA
(in Arabic)
I'm hungry!

48   AHMED
(in Arabic)
You're always hungry.

49   *Rabia shoves Ahmed playfully. This makes Ahmed back up into Sarah, who is walking down the street in the opposite direction. Sarah is wearing workout gear and headphones.*

50   SARAH
Hey, watch it!

51   AHMED
Sorry, sorry, it was her fault.

52   *Sarah brushes it off. She is about to move on when she recognizes Karima.*

53   SARAH
Karina? Hey!

54   *Karima looks at her friends and back at Sarah.*

55   RABIA
It's *Karima*.

56   SARAH
We missed you last night! Ben was totally asking about you.

57 **AHMED**
Last night?

58 *Karima flushes. Ahmed and Rabia give Karima a look like: Seriously?*

59 **KARIMA**
Thank you for inviting me. These are my friends Rabia and Ahmed. Rabia, Ahmed this is Sarah.

60 *They all look at each other, nodding awkwardly.*

61 **SARAH**
So what is this?

62 **KARIMA**
This is our other school, on the weekends. It's Arabic school.

63 **SARAH**
Double school, whoa.

64 **KARIMA**
It's actually fun.

65 **SARAH**
Cool, well hopefully we can hang out sometime. Rabia, Ahmed, it was really nice to meet you. See ya!

66 *Sarah runs off and waves. Rabia and Ahmed give Karima a look: huh, she was nice. Karima smiles.*

67 **KARIMA**
Wow. She only asked one question.

68 *They continue walking along, talking again in Arabic.*

**Scene 4** - *Karima stands alone on stage*

69 **KARIMA**
(to audience)
You know, sometimes it feels like I'm split right down the middle. There's the Karima who goes to this big loud American high school in the middle of Texas, and really wants to fit in and be normal. And then there's the one that wants to hold on to my family and my culture so tightly. And feel like I have this *place* in the world that's way bigger than me, where everyone understands me, down to my bones. These two Karimas, most of the time, feel worlds apart. Like, they don't even text each other. But then, sometimes, there's just. . .me.

NOTES

Like when I'm alone, in my room, listening to music or reading a book I really love. It's just me. And I don't feel torn at all. I just feel okay. Just like you. I guess just like everybody.

70 BLACKOUT.

Please note that excerpts and passages in the StudySync® library and this workbook are intended as touchstones to generate interest in an author's work. The excerpts and passages do not substitute for the reading of entire texts, and StudySync® strongly recommends that students seek out and purchase the whole literary or informational work in order to experience it as the author intended. Links to online resellers are available in our digital library. In addition, complete works may be ordered through an authorized reseller by filling out and returning to StudySync® the order form enclosed in this workbook.

Reading & Writing Companion    177

# First Read

Read "Karima." After you read, complete the Think Questions below.

## ☁ THINK QUESTIONS

1.  What happened to Rabia that made Karima upset?

    Karima is upset because _____.

2.  Where does Scene 2 take place?

    Scene 2 takes place _____.

3.  At the end of the play, how does Karima explain having two identities? Include evidence from the text to support your response.

    Karima says that one part of her is _____ and another part _____.

    She explains this by saying "_____."

4.  Use context to confirm the meaning of the word **assimilate** as it is used in "Karima." Write your definition of *assimilate* here.

    *Assimilate* means _____.

    A context clue is _____.

5.  What is another way to say that a message is *subtle*?

    The message is _____.

# Skill:
# Analyzing Expressions

## ★ DEFINE

When you read, you may find English expressions that you do not know. An **expression** is a group of words that communicates an idea. Three types of expressions are idioms, sayings, and figurative language. They can be difficult to understand because the meanings of the words are different from their **literal**, or usual, meanings.

An **idiom** is an expression that is commonly known among a group of people. For example, "It's raining cats and dogs" means it is raining heavily. **Sayings** are short expressions that contain advice or wisdom. For instance, "Don't count your chickens before they hatch" means do not plan on something good happening before it happens. **Figurative** language is when you describe something by comparing it with something else, either directly (using the words *like* or *as*) or indirectly. For example, "I'm as hungry as a horse" means I'm very hungry. None of the expressions are about actual animals.

## ••• CHECKLIST FOR ANALYZING EXPRESSIONS

To determine the meaning of an expression, remember the following:

✓ If you find a confusing group of words, it may be an expression. The meaning of words in expressions may not be their literal meaning.

  • Ask yourself: Is this confusing because the words are new? Or because the words do not make sense together?

✓ Determining the overall meaning may require that you use one or more of the following:

  • context clues

  • a dictionary or other resource

  • teacher or peer support

✓ Highlight important information before and after the expression to look for clues.

Please note that excerpts and passages in the StudySync® library and this workbook are intended as touchstones to generate interest in an author's work. The excerpts and passages do not substitute for the reading of entire texts, and StudySync® strongly recommends that students seek out and purchase the whole literary or informational work in order to experience it as the author intended. Links to online resellers are available in our digital library. In addition, complete works may be ordered through an authorized reseller by filling out and returning to StudySync® the order form enclosed in this workbook.

Reading & Writing Companion

179

## ↻ YOUR TURN

Read paragraph 69 from the text. Then, using the Checklist on the previous page, answer the multiple-choice questions below.

---

from **"Karima"**

**Scene 4** - *Karima stands alone on stage*

KARIMA
(to audience)
(1) You know, sometimes it feels like I'm split right down the middle. (2) There's the Karima who goes to this big loud American high school in the middle of Texas, and really wants to fit in and be normal. (3) And then there's the one that wants to hold on to my family and my culture so tightly. (4) And I feel like I have this place in the world that's way bigger than me, where everyone understands me, down to my bones. (5) These two Karimas, most of the time, feel worlds apart. (6) Like, they don't even text each other. (7) But then, sometimes, there's just...me. (8) Like when I'm alone, in my room, listening to music or reading a book I really love. (9) It's just me. (10) And I don't feel torn at all. (11) I just feel okay. (12) Just like you. (13) I guess just like everybody.

---

1. In sentence 2, the expression "fit in" most closely means —

   ○ A. to act out in an angry way

   ○ B. to be in harmony with others

   ○ C. to wear the right sized clothes

   ○ D. to be physically active

2. When Karima says that she "wants to hold on to my family and my culture so tightly" in sentence 3, what does she mean?

   ○ A. She wants to literally hold her family and culture tightly.

   ○ B. Karima wants to stay connected to her family and culture.

   ○ C. Karima thinks that she should copy Anglo-American culture.

   ○ D. She thinks that hugging family members is a good thing.

3. If people are "worlds apart" (sentence 5), it means that they—

   ○ A. live on different hemispheres
   ○ B. live far away from each other
   ○ C. cannot understand each other
   ○ D. seem different from each other

4. When Karima says "I don't feel torn" (sentence 10), what does she mean?

   ○ A. She feels focused and whole.
   ○ B. She feels well-dressed.
   ○ C. She feels uninjured.
   ○ D. She feels like a book character.

Please note that excerpts and passages in the StudySync® library and this workbook are intended as touchstones to generate interest in an author's work. The excerpts and passages do not substitute for the reading of entire texts, and StudySync® strongly recommends that students seek out and purchase the whole literary or informational work in order to experience it as the author intended. Links to online resellers are available in our digital library. In addition, complete works may be ordered through an authorized reseller by filling out and returning to StudySync® the order form enclosed in this workbook.

Reading & Writing Companion  181

# Skill: Analyzing and Evaluating Text

## ★ DEFINE

**Analyzing** and **evaluating** a text means reading carefully to understand the author's **purpose** and **message**. In informational texts, authors may provide information or opinions on a topic. They may be writing to inform or persuade a reader. In fictional texts, the author may be **communicating** a message or lesson through their story. They may write to entertain, or to teach the reader something about life.

Sometimes authors are clear about their message and purpose. When the message or purpose is not stated directly, readers will need to look closer at the text. Readers can use textual evidence to make inferences about what the author is trying to communicate. By analyzing and evaluating the text, you can form your own thoughts and opinions about what you read.

## ••• CHECKLIST FOR ANALYZING AND EVALUATING TEXT

In order to analyze and evaluate a text, do the following:

✓ Look for details that show why the author is writing.

- Ask yourself: Is the author trying to inform, persuade, or entertain? What are the main ideas of this text?

✓ Look for details that show what the author is trying say.

- Ask yourself: What is the author's opinion about this topic? Is there a lesson I can learn from this story?

✓ Form your own thoughts and opinions about the text.

- Ask yourself: Do I agree with the author? Does this message apply to my life?

YOUR TURN

Read paragraph 69 from the text. Then, using the Checklist on the previous page, answer the multiple-choice questions below.

from **"Karima"**

**Scene 4** - *Karima stands alone on stage*

KARIMA
(to audience)
You know, sometimes it feels like I'm split right down the middle. There's the Karima who goes to this big loud American high school in the middle of Texas, and really wants to fit in and be normal. And then there's the one that wants to hold on to my family and my culture so tightly. And feel like I have this place in the world that's way bigger than me, where everyone understands me, down to my bones. These two Karimas, most of the time, feel worlds apart. Like, they don't even text each other. But then, sometimes, there's just...me. Like when I'm alone, in my room, listening to music or reading a book I really love. It's just me. And I don't feel torn at all. I just feel okay. Just like you. I guess just like everybody.

1. Repetition of the phrase "just me" serves to—

   ○ A. remind the audience that this is a play about a student named Karima

   ○ B. show how Karima likes to spend her time alone with books or music

   ○ C. show that Karima has an identity independent of how others see her

   ○ D. demonstrate how minor Karima's problems are compared to her parents

2. How can you tell that this excerpt is narrative text?

   ○ A. It features debatable opinions in addition to facts.

   ○ B. It tells a story and gives a character's point of view.

   ○ C. It requires the reader to choose one side of a debate.

   ○ D. It gives information about a topic related to history.

Reading & Writing
Companion

3. How does this aside from Karima support the author's purpose?

   ○ A. It illustrates how Karima feels pressure to fit into two cultures.

   ○ B. It shows that Texans are friendly and welcoming of immigrants.

   ○ C. It indicates that the world is bigger than just one high school.

   ○ D. It reveals that the narrator is not alone in being bullied.

4. How might asides like this one make the audience feel?

   ○ A. surprised by the break in the dialogue

   ○ B. annoyed at having to hear a lecture

   ○ C. amused by Karima's foolishness

   ○ D. involved in Karima's world

# Close Read

## ✏ WRITE

LITERARY ANALYSIS: In this drama, the main character finds herself being one way around her Arab friends and another way around her American high school peers. How does Karima express the idea of having different identities? Look at what she says and how she acts around these two peer groups. Use details and evidence from the text to support your response. Pay attention to and edit for negatives and contractions.

**Use the checklist below to guide you as you write.**

☐ What are Karima's two identities?

☐ What does Karima say to the audience that shows her two identities?

☐ What does Karima say and do around her peers to show that she has two identities?

**Use the sentence frames to organize and write your literary analysis.**

In the play "Karima," the main character has two _____.

Karima says she wants to fit in with her American _____

when she tells Sarah and Courtney that she would like to attend their party, but she _____.

Karima shows that she respects her Palestinian _____

when she acts _____ to introduce her Arab friends to Sarah.

At the end of the play, Karima says that when she's by herself she _____

have to think about trying to fit in with (anyone / no one).

PHOTO/IMAGE CREDITS:

cover, ©iStock.com/ooyoo

cover, ©iStock.com/eyewave, ©iStock.com/subjug, ©iStock.com/Ivantsov, iStock.com/borchee, ©iStock.com/seb_ra

p. iii, iStock.com/DNY59
p. iv, iStock.com/DWalker44
p. v, iStock.com/DWalker44
p. v, iStock.com/deimagine
p. vi, iStock.com/DWalker44
p. vi, ©iStock.com/halbergman
p. vi, iStock.com/DragonImages
p. vi, iStock.com/Petar Chernaev
p. vi, iStock.com/Kirby Hamilton
p. vi, iStock.com/EricFerguson
p. vii, iStock.com/hanibaram, iStock.com/seb_ra, iStock.com/Martin Barraud
p. ix, ©iStock.com/ooyoo
p. x, Nikolai Gogol - DE AGOSTINI PICTURE LIBRARY/Contributor/De Agostini/Getty Images
p. x, Gabriel García Marquez - Ulf Andersen/Contributor/Hulton Archive/Getty Images
p. x, Saronjini Naidu - Imagno/Contributor/Hulton Archive/Getty Images
p. x, Louis Pasteur - iStock.com/ilbusca
p. x, Anna Quindlen - Bobby Bank/Contributor/WireImage/Getty Images
p. xi, Najla Said - Gonzalo Marroquin/Contributor/Patrick McMullan/Getty Images
p. xi, Amy Tan - Mark Mainz/Staff/Getty Images Entertainment
p. xi, Ursula Villarreal-Moura - Used by permission of Ursula Villarreal-Moura
p. 0, ©iStock.com/francescoch
p. 2, Lipnitzki/Roger Viollet/Getty Images
p. 3, Geoffrey Clements/Corbis Historical/Getty Images
p. 5, ©iStock.com/francescoch
p. 6, ©iStock.com/DenisTangneyJr
p. 9, ©istock.com/filmfoto
p. 10, PA Images/PA Images/Getty Images
p. 11, iStock.com/adaniloff
p. 23, iStock.com/adaniloff
p. 24, iStock.com/urbancow
p. 25, iStock.com/urbancow
p. 26, iStock.com/adaniloff
p. 27, ©istock.com/Anastasiia Shavshyna
p. 28–39, The Best We Could Do by Thi Bui. Copyright © 2017 Thi Bui. Used with the permission of Express Permissions on behalf of Abrams ComicArts, an imprint of Harry N. Abrams, Inc., New York. All rights reserved. www.abramsbooks.com.
p. 40, ©istock.com/Anastasiia Shavshyna
p. 41, iStock.com/Hohenhaus
p. 42, iStock.com/Hohenhaus
p. 43, ©istock.com/Anastasiia Shavshyna
p. 44, ©iStock.com/DNY59
p. 45, iStock/ilbusca
p. 47, ©istock.com/Rike_
p. 54, ©istock.com/Rike_
p. 55, iStock.com/yipengge
p. 56, iStock.com/yipengge
p. 57, iStock.com/

p. 58, iStock.com/
p. 59, ©istock.com/Rike_
p. 60, ©istock.com/majaiva
p. 61, De Agostini Picture Library/De Agostini/Getty Images
p. 85, ©istock.com/mihtiander
p. 89, ©istock.com/mihtiander
p. 90, iStock.com/fotogaby
p. 91, iStock.com/fotogaby
p. 92, iStock.com/
p. 93, iStock.com/
p. 94, ©iStock.com/DNY59
p. 95, ©iStock.com/DNY59
p. 96, ©istock.com/mihtiander
p. 97, ©istock.com/loeskieboom
p. 101, istock.com/m-gucci
p. 106, ©iStock.com/bingokid
p. 108, George Rose/Getty Images News/Getty Images
p. 110, iStock/PepiteVoyage
p. 111, TPG/Getty Images News/Getty Images
p. 113, ©iStock.com/bingokid
p. 114, iStock.com/urbancow
p. 115, iStock.com/urbancow
p. 116, ©iStock.com/bingokid
p. 117, iStock.com/hanibaram, iStock.com/seb_ra, iStock.com/Martin Barraud
p. 118, iStock.com/Martin Barraud
p. 120, StudySync
p. 122, iStock.com/FrankvandenBergh
p. 126, iStock.com/koya79
p. 129, iStock.com/Mutlu Kurtbas
p. 132, iStock.com/DNY59
p. 135, iStock.com/Martin Barraud
p. 140, iStock.com/SKrow
p. 142, iStock.com/horiyan
p. 144, iStock.com/tofumax
p. 146, iStock.com/me4o
p. 148, iStock.com/Martin Barraud
p. 151, iStock.com/Customdesigner
p. 153, iStock.com/
p. 155, iStock.com/
p. 157, iStock.com/Martin Barraud
p. 159, ©iStock.com/julianwphoto
p. 160, iStock.com/djedzura
p. 160, iStock.com/GomezDavid
p. 160, iStock.com/
p. 160, iStock.com/jcarroll-images
p. 160, iStock.com/KatarzynaBialasiewicz
p. 162, Public Domain
p. 163, ©iStock.com/julianwphoto
p. 164, iStock.com/BlackJack3D
p. 166, ©iStock.com/AlexandrBognat
p. 168, ©iStock.com/julianwphoto
p. 169, ©iStock.com/WichitS
p. 170, iStock.com/william87
p. 170, iStock.com/Image Source
p. 170, iStock.com/GomezDavid
p. 170, iStock.com/adamkaz
p. 178, ©iStock.com/WichitS
p. 179, iStock.com/Ales_Utovko
p. 182, iStock.com/kyoshino
p. 185, ©iStock.com/WichitS

# studysync

## Text Fulfillment Through StudySync

If you are interested in specific titles, please fill out the form below and we will check availability through our partners.

## ORDER DETAILS

Date:

| TITLE | AUTHOR | Paperback/ Hardcover | Specific Edition *If Applicable* | Quantity |
|-------|--------|----------------------|----------------------------------|----------|
|  |  |  |  |  |
|  |  |  |  |  |
|  |  |  |  |  |
|  |  |  |  |  |
|  |  |  |  |  |
|  |  |  |  |  |
|  |  |  |  |  |
|  |  |  |  |  |

### SHIPPING INFORMATION

Contact:

Title:

School/District:

Address Line 1:

Address Line 2:

Zip or Postal Code:

Phone:

Mobile:

Email:

### BILLING INFORMATION ☐ *SAME AS SHIPPING*

Contact:

Title:

School/District:

Address Line 1:

Address Line 2:

Zip or Postal Code:

Phone:

Mobile:

Email:

### PAYMENT INFORMATION

☐ CREDIT CARD

Name on Card:

Card Number:     Expiration Date:     Security Code:

☐ PO

Purchase Order Number:

StudySync Text Fulfillment, BookheadEd Learning, LLC
610 Daniel Young Drive | Sonoma, CA 95476